AS YOU LIKE IT

AS YOU LIKE IT

William Shakespeare

WORDSWORTH CLASSICS

The paper in this book is produced from pure wood
pulp, without the use of chlorine or any other substance
harmful to the environment. The energy used in its
production consists almost entirely of hydroelectricity
and heat generated from waste materials, thereby
conserving fossil fuels and contributing little to the
greenhouse effect.

This edition published 1993 by
Wordsworth Editions Limited
8B East Street, Ware, Hertfordshire SG12 9HJ

ISBN 1 85326 0592

Printed and bound in Denmark by Nørhaven

INTRODUCTION

As You Like It is a romantic pastoral comedy largely based on Thomas Lodge's *Rosalyne: Euphues Golden Legacy* which had been published in 1590. Although it was first registered in 1599, it is likely that Shakespeare's play was actually written some years earlier, and it was first printed in the First Folio of 1623.

Duke Frederick has banished his brother, the rightful Duke, to the Forest of Arden with a group of his faithful followers. The real Duke's daughter Rosalind and Frederick's daughter Celia are devoted cousins. They are resident at Frederick's court, and when Rosalind sees the young man Orlando defeat Frederick's champion in a wrestling match she falls in love with him. Frederick is jealous of Rosalind's accomplishments and banishes her; she goes to the Forest of Arden disguised as the youth Ganymede, accompanied by Celia who takes the name of Aliena and the court jester Touchstone. Orlando, too, flees to the Forest driven there by the tyrannical behaviour of his elder brother Oliver. Though Orlando had fallen in love with Rosalind after the wrestling match, he does not succeed in penetrating Ganymede's disguise when they meet, and confesses his love for Rosalind to Ganymede. Meanwhile, Oliver comes to the Forest, and when Orlando saves him from a lioness, the brothers are reconciled. The pace of romantic couplings increases with Touchstone wooing Audrey, a country wench, Oliver wooing Celia, the shepherd Silvius woos the shepherdess Phebe who in turn woos the disguised Rosalind, thinking her to be a man. At last Rosalind reveals her identity, the four pairs of lovers are united in the Feast of Hymen before the banished Duke and his followers. Finally, it is announced that Frederick has become a monk, and that the Duke and his followers may resume what is rightfully theirs.

In spite of the inadequacies of the plot, *As You Like It* is second only to *Twelfth Night* in comic accomplishment. Shakespeare manages to mock the conventions of romantic love in Ganymede's exchanges with Orlando, pastoral convention in his depiction of Silvius and Phebe, pragmatic wooing in the case of Touchstone and Audrey while maintaining the romance of the genuine love of

Rosalind and Orlando. The sententiousness of the fashionable courtier is captured in Jaques, one of the Duke's attendants, whose melancholy moralizing satirizes current intellectual fashion, and the many songs add another layer of delight to this frothy entertainment.

Details of William Shakespeare's early life are scanty. He was the son of a prosperous merchant of Stratford upon Avon, and tradition has it that he was born on 23rd April 1564; records show that he was baptized three days later. It is likely that he attended the local Grammar School, but had no university education. Of his early career there is no record, though John Aubrey states that he was a country schoolmaster. How he became involved with the stage is equally uncertain, but he was sufficiently established as a playwright by 1592 to be criticized in print. He was a leading member of the Lord Chamberlain's Company, which became the King's Men on the accession of James I in 1603. Shakespeare married Anne Hathaway in 1582, by whom he had two daughters and a son, Hamnet, who died in 1586. Towards the end of his life he loosened his ties with London, and retired to New Place, his substantial property in Stratford which he had bought in 1597. He died on 23rd April 1616 aged 52, and is buried in Holy Trinity Church, Stratford.

Further reading:

B O Bonazza: Shakespeare's Early Comedies: A Structural Analysis 1966
J R Brown: Shakespeare and His Comedies revised edition 1962
B Evans: Shakespeare's Comedies 1962
H Felperin: Shakespearean Romance 1973
P G Philias: Shakespeare's Romantic Comedies 1966

The scene: Oliver's house, Duke Frederick's court, and the Forest of Arden

CHARACTERS IN THE PLAY

A banished DUKE

FREDERICK, *his brother, and usurper of his dominions*

AMIENS
JAQUES } *lords attending on the banished Duke*

LE BEAU, *a courtier attending upon Frederick*

CHARLES, *wrestler to Frederick*

OLIVER
JAQUES } *sons of Sir Rowland de Boys*
ORLANDO

ADAM
DENNIS } *servants to Oliver*

TOUCHSTONE, *a clown*

SIR OLIVER MARTEXT, *a vicar*

CORIN
SILVIUS } *shepherds*

WILLIAM, *a country fellow, in love with Audrey*

A person representing Hymen

ROSALIND, *daughter to the banished Duke*

CELIA, *daughter to Frederick*

PHEBE, *a shepherdess*

AUDREY, *a country wench*

Lords, pages, foresters, and attendants

AS YOU LIKE IT

An orchard, near Oliver's house

ORLANDO *and* ADAM

Orlando. As I remember, Adam, it was upon this fashion: a' bequeathed me by will but poor thousand crowns and, as thou say'st, charged my brother on his blessing to breed me well: and there begins my sadness...My brother Jaques he keeps at school, and report speaks goldenly of his profit: for my part, he keeps me rustically at home, or, to speak more properly, stays me here at home unkept: for call you that 'keeping' for a gentleman of my birth, that differs not from the stalling of an ox? His horses are bred better—for, besides that they are fair with their feeding, they are taught their manage, and to that end riders dearly hired: but I, his brother, gain nothing under him but growth, for the which his animals on his dunghills are as much bound to him as I...Besides this nothing that he so plentifully gives me, the something that nature gave me his countenance seems to take from me: he lets me feed with his hinds, bars me the place of a brother, and, as much as in him lies, mines my gentility with my education.... This is it, Adam, that grieves me—and the spirit of my father, which I think is within me, begins to mutiny against this servitude....I will no longer endure it, though yet I know no wise remedy how to avoid it.

OLIVER *enters the orchard*

Adam. Yonder comes my master, your brother.

Orlando. Go apart, Adam, and thou shalt hear how he will shake me up.   [*Adam withdraws a little*

Oliver. Now, sir! what make you here?

Orlando. Nothing: I am not taught to make any thing.

Oliver. What mar you then, sir?

30 *Orlando.* Marry, sir, I am helping you to mar that which God made, a poor unworthy brother of yours, with idleness.

Oliver. Marry, sir, be better employed, and be naught awhile.

Orlando. Shall I keep your hogs and eat husks with them? What prodigal portion have I spent, that I should come to such penury?

Oliver. Know you where you are, sir?

Orlando. O, sir, very well: here in your orchard.

40 *Oliver.* Know you before whom, sir?

Orlando. Ay, better than him I am before knows me...
I know you are my eldest brother, and in the gentle condition of blood you should so know me...The courtesy of nations allows you my better, in that you are the first-born, but the same tradition takes not away my blood, were there twenty brothers betwixt us: I have as much of my father in me as you, albeit I confess your coming before me is nearer to his reverence.

Oliver. What, boy! *[he strikes him*

50 *Orlando.* Come, come, elder brother, you are too young in this. *[he takes him by the throat*

Oliver. Wilt thou lay hands on me, villain?

Orlando. I am no villain: I am the youngest son of Sir Rowland de Boys, he was my father, and he is thrice a villain that says such a father begot villains...Wert thou not my brother, I would not take this hand from thy throat, till this other had pulled out thy tongue for saying so—thou hast railed on thyself. *[Adam comes forward*

Adam. Sweet masters, be patient. For your father's

60 remembrance, be at accord.

Oliver [*struggles*]. Let me go, I say.

Orlando. I will not till I please: you shall hear me… My father charged you in his will to give me good education: you have trained me like a peasant, obscuring and hiding from me all gentleman-like qualities…The spirit of my father grows strong in me, and I will no longer endure it: therefore allow me such exercises as may become a gentleman, or give me the poor allottery my father left me by testament—with that I will go buy my fortunes.   [*he releases him* 70

Oliver. And what wilt thou do? beg when that is spent? Well, sir, get you in: I will not long be troubled with you: you shall have some part of your 'will.' I pray you, leave me.

Orlando. I will no further offend you than becomes me for my good.   [*he turns to go*

Oliver. Get you with him, you old dog.

Adam. Is 'old dog' my reward? Most true, I have lost my teeth in your service…God be with my old master! he would not have spoke such a word.   80

                    [*Orlando and Adam depart*

Oliver. Is it even so? begin you to grow upon me? I will physic your rankness, and yet give no thousand crowns neither…Holla, Dennis!

DENNIS *comes from the house*

Dennis. Calls your worship?

Oliver. Was not Charles, the duke's wrestler, here to speak with me?

Dennis. So please you, he is here at the door, and importunes access to you.

Oliver. Call him in…[*Dennis goes*] 'Twill be a good way…and to-morrow the wrestling is.   90

DENNIS returns, bringing CHARLES

Charles. Good morrow to your worship.

Oliver. Good Monsieur Charles...[*they salute*] What's
the new news at the new court?

Charles. There's no news at the court, sir, but the old
news: that is, the old duke is banished by his younger
brother the new duke, and three or four loving lords
have put themselves into voluntary exile with him, whose
lands and revenues enrich the new duke, therefore he
gives them good leave to wander.

100 *Oliver.* Can you tell if Rosalind, the duke's daughter,
be banished with her father?

Charles. O, no; for the duke's daughter, her cousin,
so loves her—being ever from their cradles bred together—that she would have followed her exile, or have
died to stay behind her...She is at the court, and no less
beloved of her uncle than his own daughter—and never
two ladies loved as they do.

Oliver. Where will the old duke live?

Charles. They say he is already in the forest of Arden,
110 and a many merry men with him; and there they live
like the old Robin Hood of England: they say many
young gentlemen flock to him every day, and fleet the
time carelessly as they did in the golden world.

Oliver. What, you wrestle to-morrow before the new
duke?

Charles. Marry, do I, sir: and I came to acquaint you
with a matter...I am given, sir, secretly to understand
that your younger brother, Orlando, hath a disposition
to come in disguised against me to try a fall: to-morrow,
120 sir, I wrestle for my credit, and he that escapes me without some broken limb shall acquit him well: your brother
is but young and tender, and for your love I would be

loath to foil him, as I must for my own honour if he
come in: therefore, out of my love to you, I came hither
to acquaint you withal, that either you might stay him
from his intendment, or brook such disgrace well as he
shall run into, in that it is a thing of his own search, and
altogether against my will.

Oliver. Charles, I thank thee for thy love to me, which
thou shalt find I will most kindly requite...I had myself 130
notice of my brother's purpose herein, and have by
underhand means laboured to dissuade him from it; but
he is resolute....I'll tell thee, Charles—it is the stubborn-
est young fellow of France, full of ambition, an envious
emulator of every man's good parts, a secret and villanous contriver against me his natural brother: therefore use thy discretion, I had as lief thou didst break his
neck as his finger....And thou wert best look to't; for if
thou dost him any slight disgrace, or if he do not
mightily grace himself on thee, he will practise against 140
thee by poison, entrap thee by some treacherous device,
and never leave thee till he hath ta'en thy life by some
indirect means or other: for, I assure thee (and almost
with tears I speak it), there is not one so young, and so
villanous this day living....I speak but brotherly of him,
but should I anatomize him to thee as he is, I must blush
and weep, and thou must look pale and wonder.

Charles. I am heartily glad I came hither to you...If
he come to-morrow, I'll give him his payment: if ever
he go alone again, I'll never wrestle for prize more: and 150
so, God keep your worship!

Oliver. Farewell, good Charles....[*Charles takes his
leave*] Now will I stir this gamester: I hope I shall see
an end of him; for my soul (yet I know not why) hates
nothing more than he...Yet he's gentle, never schooled
and yet learned, full of noble device, of all sorts en-

chantingly beloved, and indeed so much in the heart.of
the world, and especially of my own people, who best
know him, that I am altogether misprized: but it shall
160 not be so long—this wrestler shall clear all...Nothing
remains but that I kindle the boy thither, which now I'll
go about. [*he goes within*

[1. 2.] *A lawn near the palace of Duke Frederick*
ROSALIND *and* CELIA, *seated*

Celia. I pray thee, Rosalind, sweet my coz, be merry.

Rosalind. Dear Celia, I show more mirth than I am
mistress of, and would you yet I were merrier? Unless you
could teach me to forget a banished father, you must not
learn me how to remember any extraordinary pleasure.

Celia. Herein, I see, thou lov'st me not with the full
weight that I love thee; if my uncle, thy banished father,
had banished thy uncle, the duke my father, so thou
hadst been still with me, I could have taught my love
10 to take thy father for mine; so wouldst thou, if the truth
of thy love to me were so righteously tempered as mine
is to thee.

Rosalind. Well, I will forget the condition of my estate,
to rejoice in yours.

Celia. You know my father hath no child but I, nor
none is like to have; and truly when he dies, thou shalt
be his heir: for what he hath taken away from thy father
perforce, I will render thee again in affection...by mine
honour I will, and when I break that oath, let me turn
20 monster: therefore, my sweet Rose, my dear Rose, be
merry.

Rosalind. From henceforth I will, coz, and devise
sports...Let me see—what think you of falling in love?

Celia. Marry, I prithee, do, to make sport withal: but
love no man in good earnest, nor no further in sport

neither, than with safety of a pure blush thou mayst in honour come off again.

Rosalind. What shall be our sport then?

Celia. Let us sit and mock the good housewife Fortune from her wheel, that her gifts may henceforth 30 be bestowed equally.

Rosalind. I would we could do so; for her benefits are mightily misplaced, and the bountiful blind woman doth most mistake in her gifts to women.

Celia. 'Tis true, for those that she makes fair she scarce makes honest, and those that she makes honest she makes very ill-favouredly.

Rosalind. Nay, now thou goest from Fortune's office to Nature's: Fortune reigns in gifts of the world, not in the lineaments of Nature.   40

TOUCHSTONE *approaches*

Celia. No? When Nature hath made a fair creature, may she not by Fortune fall into the fire? Though Nature hath given us wit to flout at Fortune, hath not Fortune sent in this fool to cut off the argument?

Rosalind. Indeed, there is Fortune too hard for Nature, when Fortune makes Nature's natural the cutter-off of Nature's wit.

Celia. Peradventure this is not Fortune's work neither, but Nature's, who perceiveth our natural wits too dull to reason of such goddesses and hath sent this natural for our 50 whetstone: for always the dulness of the fool is the whetstone of the wits....How now, wit! whither wander you?

Touchstone. Mistress, you must come away to your father.

Celia. Were you made the messenger?

Touchstone. No, by mine honour, but I was bid to come for you.

Rosalind. Where learned you that oath, fool?

Touchstone. Of a certain knight, that swore by his
60 honour they were good pancakes, and swore by his
honour the mustard was naught: now I'll stand to it,
the pancakes were naught and the mustard was good,
and yet was not the knight forsworn.

Celia. How prove you that, in the great heap of your
knowledge?

Rosalind. Ay, marry, now unmuzzle your wisdom.

Touchstone. Stand you both forth now: stroke your
chins, and swear by your beards that I am a knave.

Celia. By our beards (if we had them) thou art.

70 *Touchstone.* By my knavery (if I had it) then I were:
but if you swear by that that is not, you are not forsworn:
no more was this knight, swearing by his honour, for he
never had any; or if he had, he had sworn it away,
before ever he saw those pancakes or that mustard.

Celia. Prithee, who is't that thou mean'st?

Touchstone [*to Rosalind*]. One that old †Frederick,
your father, loves.

Rosalind. My father's love is enough to honour him.
Enough! speak no more of him—you'll be whipped for
80 taxation one of these days.

Touchstone. The more pity, that fools may not speak
wisely what wise men do foolishly.

Celia. By my troth, thou sayest true: for since the little
wit that fools have was silenced, the little foolery that
wise men have makes a great show...Here comes
Monsieur Le Beau.

LE BEAU is seen hurrying towards them

Rosalind. With his mouth full of news.

Celia. Which he will put on us, as pigeons feed their
young.

Rosalind. Then shall we be news-crammed.   90

Celia. All the better: we shall be the more marketable. Bon jour, Monsieur Le Beau! what's the news?

Le Beau. Fair princess, you have lost much good sport.

Celia. Sport? Of what colour?

Le Beau. What colour, madam? How shall I answer you?

Rosalind. As wit and fortune will.

Touchstone [*mocking him*]. Or as the Destinies decree.

Celia. Well said, that was laid on with a trowel.

Touchstone. Nay, if I keep not my rank—   100

Rosalind. Thou losest thy old smell.

Le Beau. You amaze me, ladies: I would have told you of good wrestling, which you have lost the sight of.

Rosalind. Yet tell us the manner of the wrestling.

Le Beau. I will tell you the beginning, and, if it please your ladyships, you may see the end—for the best is yet to do, and here, where you are, they are coming to perform it.

Celia. Well, the beginning, that is dead and buried?

Le Beau. There comes an old man and his three sons—   110

Celia. I could match this beginning with an old tale.

Le Beau. Three proper young men, of excellent growth and presence.

Rosalind. With bills on their necks: 'Be it known unto all men by these presents.'

Le Beau. The eldest of the three wrestled with Charles, the duke's wrestler, which Charles in a moment threw him and broke three of his ribs, that there is little hope of life in him: so he served the second, and so the third… Yonder they lie, the poor old man their father making   120 such pitiful dole over them that all the beholders take his part with weeping.

Rosalind. Alas!

Touchstone. But what is the sport, monsieur, that the ladies have lost?

Le Beau. Why, this that I speak of.

Touchstone. Thus men may grow wiser every day. It is the first time that ever I heard breaking of ribs was sport for ladies.

130 *Celia.* Or I, I promise thee.

Rosalind. But is there any else longs to see this broken music in his sides? is there yet another dotes upon rib-breaking? Shall we see this wrestling, cousin?

Le Beau. You must if you stay here, for here is the place appointed for the wrestling, and they are ready to perform it.

Celia. Yonder, sure, they are coming....Let us now stay and see it.

A flourish of trumpets. Duke FREDERICK with his lords, ORLANDO, CHARLES, and attendants cross the lawn towards a plot prepared for the wrestling

Duke Frederick. Come on. Since the youth will not
140 be entreated, his own peril on his forwardness.

Rosalind. Is yonder the man?

Le Beau. Even he, madam.

Celia. Alas, he is too young: yet he looks successfully.

Duke Frederick. How now, daughter and cousin! are you crept hither to see the wrestling?

Rosalind. Ay, my liege, so please you give us leave.

Duke Frederick. You will take little delight in it, I can tell you, there is such odds in the man...In pity of the challenger's youth I would fain dissuade him, but he
150 will not be entreated....Speak to him, ladies—see if you can move him.

Celia. Call him hither, good Monsieur Le Beau.

Duke Frederick. Do so: I'll not be by. [*he takes his seat*

Le Beau. Monsieur the challenger, the princess calls·
for you.

Orlando [*comes forward*]. I attend them with all respect and duty.

Rosalind. Young man, have you challenged Charles
the wrestler?

Orlando [*bows*]. No, fair princess: he is the general 160
challenger. I come but in, as others do, to try with him
the strength of my youth.

Celia. Young gentleman, your spirits are too bold for
your years...You have seen cruel proof of this man's
strength. If you saw yourself with your eyes, or knew
yourself with your judgement, the fear of your adventure would counsel you to a more equal enterprise....
We pray you, for your own sake, to embrace your own
safety, and give over this attempt.

Rosalind. Do, young sir, your reputation shall not 170
therefore be misprized: we will make it our suit to the
duke that the wrestling might not go forward.

Orlando. I beseech you, punish me not with your hard
thoughts, wherein I confess me much guilty to deny so
fair and excellent ladies any thing. But let your fair eyes
and gentle wishes go with me to my trial: wherein if I
be foiled, there is but one shamed that was never
gracious; if killed, but one dead that is willing to be so:
I shall do my friends no wrong, for I have none to
lament me; the world no injury, for in it I have nothing: 180
only in the world I fill up a place, which may be better
supplied when I have made it empty.

Rosalind. The little strength that I have, I would it
were with you.

Celia. And mine, to eke out hers.

Rosalind. Fare you well...Pray heaven, I be deceived
in you!

Celia. Your heart's desires be with you!

Charles [calls]. Come, where is this young gallant that
190 is so desirous to lie with his mother earth?

Orlando. Ready, sir, but his will hath in it a more
modest working.

Duke Frederick. You shall try but one fall.

Charles. No, I warrant your grace, you shall not entreat him to a second, that have so mightily persuaded
him from a first.

Orlando. An you mean to mock me after, you should
not have mocked me before: but come your ways.

Rosalind. Now, Hercules be thy speed, young man!
200 *Celia.* I would I were invisible, to catch the strong
fellow by the leg.

> [*The wrestling begins: they close, Orlando
> skilfully securing the better hold*

Rosalind. O excellent young man!

Celia. If I had a thunderbolt in mine eye, I can tell
who should down.

[*The wrestlers sway and strain to and fro, till of a sudden
Charles is thrown heavily to the ground; a great shout*
Duke Frederick [rises]. No more, no more.

Orlando. Yes, I beseech your grace—I am not yet well
breathed.

Duke Frederick. How dost thou, Charles?

Le Beau.   He cannot speak, my lord.

Duke Frederick. Bear him away...

> [*they take up Charles and carry him forth*
> What is thy name, young man?

210 *Orlando.* Orlando, my liege; the youngest son of Sir
Rowland de Boys.

Duke Frederick. I would thou hadst been son to some
man else.

The world esteemed thy father honourable,

But I did find him still mine enemy:
Thou shouldst have better pleased me with this deed,
Hadst thou descended from another house:
But fare thee well, thou art a gallant youth.
I would thou hadst told me of another father.
  [*Duke Frederick, Le Beau and the other lords depart*
  Celia. Were I my father, coz, would I do this?
  Orlando. I am more proud to be Sir Rowland's son,   220
His youngest son, and would not change that calling,
To be adopted heir to Frederick.
  Rosalind. My father loved Sir Rowland as his soul,
And all the world was of my father's mind.
Had I before known this young man his son,
I should have given him tears unto entreaties,
Ere he should thus have ventured.
  Celia.   Gentle cousin,
Let us go thank him, and encourage him:
My father's rough and envious disposition
Sticks me at heart...[*they rise and accost Orlando*] Sir,
      you have well deserved.   230
If you do keep your promises in love
But justly as you have exceeded promise,
Your mistress shall be happy.
  Rosalind [*takes a chain from her neck*] Gentleman,
Wear this for me...one out of suits with fortune,
That could give more, but that her hand lacks means....
Shall we go, coz?   [*she turns and walks away*
  Celia [*follows*]. Ay: fare you well, fair gentleman.
  Orlando. Can I not say, 'I thank you'? My better
      parts
Are all thrown down, and that which here stands up
Is but a quintain, a mere lifeless block. '
  Rosalind. He calls us back: my pride fell with my
      fortunes—   240

I'll ask him what he would...[*she turns again*] Did you
    call, sir?
Sir, you have wrestled well and overthrown
More than your enemies.   [*they gaze upon each other*
   Celia [*plucks her sleeve*] Will you go, coz?
   Rosalind. Have with you...Fare you well.
              [*she hastens away, Celia following*
   Orlando. What passion hangs these weights upon my
    tongue?
I cannot speak to her, yet she urged conference.

LE BEAU *returns*

O poor Orlando, thou art overthrown!
Or Charles, or something weaker, masters thee.
   Le Beau. Good sir, I do in friendship counsel you
250 To leave this place...Albeit you have deserved
High commendation, true applause, and love,
Yet such is now the duke's condition,
That he misconstrues all that you have done...
The duke is humorous—what he is, indeed,
More suits you to conceive than I to speak of.
   Orlando. I thank you, sir: and, pray you, tell me this,
Which of the two was daughter of the duke,
That here was at the wrestling?
   Le Beau. Neither his daughter, if we judge by manners,
260 But yet, indeed, the smaller is his daughter.
The other is daughter to the banished duke,
And here detained by her usurping uncle,
To keep his daughter company—whose loves
Are dearer than the natural bond of sisters...
But I can tell you that of late this duke
Hath ta'en displeasure 'gainst his gentle niece,
Grounded upon no other argument
But that the people praise her for her virtues,

And pity her for her good father's sake;
And, on my life, his malice 'gainst the lady   270
Will suddenly break forth...Sir, fare you well.
Hereafter, in a better world than this,
I shall desire more love and knowledge of you.

  Orlando. I rest much bounden to you: fare you well....

[Le Beau goes

Thus must I from the smoke into the smother,
From tyrant duke unto a tyrant brother....
But heavenly Rosalind!   [*he departs, musing*

[1. 3.]   *A room in the palace of Duke Frederick*

ROSALIND *on a couch with her face to the wall,* CELIA
bending over her

  Celia. Why cousin, why Rosalind...Cupid have
mercy! Not a word?

  Rosalind. Not one to throw at a dog.

  Celia. No, thy words are too precious to be cast away
upon curs, throw some of them at me; come, lame me
with reasons.

  Rosalind. Then there were two cousins laid up, when
the one should be lamed with reasons, and the other
mad without any.

  Celia. But is all this for your father?   10

  Rosalind. No, some of it is for my child's father...
[*rises*] O, how full of briars is this working-day world!

  Celia. They are but burs, cousin, thrown upon thee
in holiday foolery. If we walk not in the trodden paths,
our very petticoats will catch them.

  Rosalind. I could shake them off my coat—these burs
are in my heart.

  Celia. Hem them away.

Rosalind. I would try, if I could cry 'hem' and have
20 him.

Celia. Come, come, wrestle with thy affections.

Rosalind. O, they take the part of a better wrestler
than myself.

Celia. O, a good wish upon you! you will try in time,
in despite of a fall....But turning these jests out of service, let us talk in good earnest: is it possible, on such
a sudden, you should fall into so strong a liking with old
Sir Rowland's youngest son?

Rosalind. The duke my father loved his father dearly.

30 *Celia.* Doth it therefore ensue that you should love
his son dearly? By this kind of chase, I should hate
him, for my father hated his father dearly; yet I hate
not Orlando.

Rosalind. No, faith, hate him not, for my sake.

Celia. Why should I not? doth he not deserve well?

Rosalind. Let me love him for that, and do you love
him because I do....[*the door is flung open and* DUKE
FREDERICK *enters, preceded by attendants and the lords
of his council*] Look, here comes the duke.

40 *Celia.* With his eyes full of anger.

Duke Frederick [*pausing in the doorway*]. Mistress,
     dispatch you with your safest haste
And get you from our court.

Rosalind.   Me, uncle?

Duke Frederick.   You, cousin.
Within these ten days if that thou be'st found
So near our public court as twenty miles,
Thou diest for it.

Rosalind.   I do beseech your grace,
Let me the knowledge of my fault bear with me:
If with myself I hold intelligence
Or have acquaintance with mine own desires,

If that I do not dream or be not frantic—
As I do trust I am not—then, dear uncle,   50
Never so much as in a thought unborn
Did I offend your highness.

  Duke Frederick.   Thus do all traitors!
If their purgation did consist in words,
They are as innocent as grace itself:
Let it suffice thee that I trust thee not.

  Rosalind. Yet your mistrust cannot make me a traitor:
Tell me whereon the likelihood depends.

  Duke Frederick. Thou art thy father's daughter, there's
    enough.

  Rosalind. So was I when your highness took his
    dukedom,
So was I when your highness banished him;   60
Treason is not inherited, my lord,
Or, if we did derive it from our friends,
What's that to me? my father was no traitor.
Then, good my liege, mistake me not so much
To think my poverty is treacherous.

  Celia. Dear sovereign, hear me speak.

  Duke Frederick. Ay, Celia, we stayed her for your
    sake,
Else had she with her father ranged along.

  Celia. I did not then entreat to have her stay,
It was your pleasure and your own remorse.   70
I was too young that time to value her,
But now I know her: if she be a traitor,
Why so am I: we still have slept together,
Rose at an instant, learned, played, eat together,
And wheresoe'er we went, like Juno's swans,
Still we went coupled and inseparable.

  Duke Frederick. She is too subtle for thee, and her
    smoothness,

Her very silence and her patience
Speak to the people, and they pity her...
80 Thou art a fool—she robs thee of thy name,
And thou wilt show more bright and seem more virtuous
When she is gone: then open not thy lips.
Firm and irrevocable is my doom
Which I have passed upon her—she is banished.
  Celia. Pronounce that sentence then on me, my liege,
I cannot live out of her company.
  Duke Frederick. You are a fool...You, niece, provide
    yourself.
If you outstay the time, upon mine honour,
And in the greatness of my word, you die.
    [*he turns and leaves the room, his lords following him*
90 *Celia.* O my poor Rosalind, whither wilt thou go?
Wilt thou change fathers? I will give thee mine...
I charge thee, be not thou more grieved than I am.
  Rosalind. I have more cause.
  Celia.   Thou hast not, cousin.
Prithee, be cheerful; know'st thou not, the duke
Hath banished me his daughter?
  Rosalind.   That he hath not.
  Celia. No, hath not? Rosalind lacks then the love
Which teacheth thee that thou and I am one.
Shall we be sundred? shall we part, sweet girl?
No, let my father seek another heir...
100 Therefore devise with me how we may fly,
Whither to go and what to bear with us,
And do not seek to take your change upon you,
To bear your griefs yourself and leave me out;
For, by this heaven, now at our sorrows pale,
Say what thou canst, I'll go along with thee.
  Rosalind. Why, whither shall we go?
  Celia. To seek my uncle in the forest of Arden.

Rosalind. Alas, what danger will it be to us,
Maids as we are, to travel forth so far!
Beauty provoketh thieves sooner than gold.   110

   Celia. I'll put myself in poor and mean attire,
And with a kind of umber smirch my face,
The like do you, so shall we pass along
And never stir assailants.

   Rosalind.   Were it not better,
Because that I am more than common tall,
That I did suit me all points like a man?
A gallant curtle-axe upon my thigh,
A boar-spear in my hand, and in my heart
Lie there what hidden woman's fear there will,
We'll have a swashing and a martial outside,   120
As many other mannish cowards have
That do outface it with their semblances.

   Celia. What shall I call thee when thou art a man?

   Rosalind. I'll have no worse a name than Jove's
     own page,
And therefore look you call me Ganymede.
But what will you be called?

   Celia. Something that hath a reference to my state;
No longer Celia, but Aliena.

   Rosalind. But, cousin, what if we assayed to steal
The clownish fool out of your father's court?   130
Would he not be a comfort to our travel?

   Celia. He'll go along o'er the wide world with me,
Leave me alone to woo him...Let's away,
And get our jewels and our wealth together,
Devise the fittest time and safest way
To hide us from pursuit that will be made
After my flight...Now go we in content
To liberty, and not to banishment.   *[they go*

[2. 1.]   *The forest of Arden*

The entrance to a cave, with a spreading tree before it.
The exiled Duke, 'AMIENS and two or three Lords like
foresters' come from the cave

 Duke. Now, my co-mates and brothers in exile,
Hath not old custom made this life more sweet
Than that of painted pomp? Are not these woods
More free from peril than the envious court?
Here feel we not the penalty of Adam,
The seasons' difference?—as the icy fang
And churlish chiding of the winter's wind,
Which, when it bites and blows upon my body,
Even till I shrink with cold, I smile and say
10 'This is no flattery: these are counsellors
That feelingly persuade me what I am'...
Sweet are the uses of adversity,
Which like the toad, ugly and venomous,
Wears yet a precious jewel in his head:
And this our life, exempt from public haunt,
Finds tongues in trees, books in the running brooks,
Sermons in stones, and good in every thing.
I would not change it.
 Amiens.   Happy is your grace,
That can translate the stubbornness of fortune
20 Into so quiet and so sweet a style.
 Duke. Come, shall we go and kill us venison?
And yet it irks me the poor dappled fools,
Being native burghers of this desert city,
Should in their own confines with forkéd heads
Have their round haunches gored.
 First Lord.   Indeed, my lord,
The melancholy Jaques grieves at that,
And, in that kind, swears you do more usurp

Than doth your brother that hath banished you:
To-day my Lord of Amiens and myself
Did steal behind him as he lay along   30
Under an oak, whose antique root peeps out
Upon the brook that brawls along this wood,
To the which place a poor sequestred stag,
That from the hunter's aim had ta'en a hurt,
Did come to languish; and, indeed, my lord,
The wretched animal heaved forth such groans,
That their discharge did stretch his leathern coat
Almost to bursting, and the big round tears
Coursed one another down his innocent nose
In piteous chase: and thus the hairy fool,   40
Much markéd of the melancholy Jaques,
Stood on th'extremest verge of the swift brook,
Augmenting it with tears.
    Duke.   But what said Jaques?
Did he not moralize this spectacle?
    First Lord. O, yes, into a thousand similes.
First, for his weeping in the needless stream;
'Poor deer,' quoth he, 'thou mak'st a testament
As worldlings do, giving thy sum of more
To that which had too much': then, being there alone,
Left and abandoned of his velvet friends;   50
'"Tis right,' quoth he, 'thus misery doth part
The flux of company': anon a careless herd,
Full of the pasture, jumps along by him
And never stays to greet him; 'Ay,' quoth Jaques,
'Sweep on, you fat and greasy citizens!
'Tis just the fashion; wherefore do you look
Upon that poor and broken bankrupt there?'
Thus most invectively he pierceth through
The body of the country, city, court,
Yea, and of this our life, swearing that we   60

Are mere usurpers, tyrants and what's worse,
To fright the animals and to kill them up
In their assigned and native dwelling-place.
  Duke. And did you leave him in this contemplation?
  Second Lord. We did, my lord, weeping and
     commenting
Upon the sobbing deer.
  Duke.   Show me the place,
I love to cope him in these sullen fits,
For then he's full of matter.
  First Lord. I'll bring you to him straight.   [*they go*

[2. 2.]   *A room in the palace of Duke Frederick*

Duke FREDERICK, *lords, and attendants*

  Duke Frederick. Can it be possible that no man
     saw them?
It cannot be. Some villains of my court
Are of consent and sufferance in this.
  First Lord. I cannot hear of any that did see her.
The ladies, her attendants of her chamber,
Saw her abed, and in the morning early
They found the bed untreasured of their mistress.
  Second Lord. My lord, the roynish clown, at whom
     so oft
Your grace was wont to laugh, is also missing.
10 Hisperia, the princess' gentlewoman,
Confesses that she secretly o'erheard
Your daughter and her cousin much commend
The parts and graces of the wrestler
That did but lately foil the sinewy Charles,
And she believes wherever they are gone
That youth is surely in their company.

Duke Frederick. Send to his brother, fetch that
    gallant hither.
If he be absent, bring his brother to me—
I'll make him find him: do this suddenly;
And let not search and inquisition quail   20
To bring again these foolish runaways.   *[they go*

[2. 3.]   *The orchard near Oliver's house*
        ORLANDO und ADAM, meeting

Orlando. Who's there?
Adam. What! my young master? O my gentle master,
O my sweet master, O you memory
Of old Sir Rowland...why, what make you here?
Why are you virtuous? Why do people love you?
And wherefore are you gentle, strong, and valiant?
Why would you be so fond to overcome
The bonny prizer of the humorous duke?
Your praise is come too swiftly home before you.
Know you not, master, to some kind of men   10
Their graces serve them but as enemies?
No more do yours; your virtues, gentle master,
Are sanctified and holy traitors to you...
O, what a world is this, when what is comely
Envenoms him that bears it!
  Orlando. Why, what's the matter?
   Adam.   O unhappy youth,
Come not within these doors; within this roof
The enemy of all your graces lives...
Your brother—no, no brother—yet the son
(Yet not the son, I will not call him son)   20
Of him I was about to call his father—
Hath heard your praises, and this night he means
To burn the lodging where you use to lie,
And you within it: if he fail of that,

He will have other means to cut you off:
I overheard him...and his practices...
This is no place, this house is but a butchery;
Abhor it, fear it, do not enter it.
  Orlando. Why, whither, Adam, wouldst thou have
    me go?
30 *Adam.* No matter whither, so you come not here.
  Orlando. What, wouldst thou have me go and beg
    my food?
Or with a base and boisterous sword enforce
A thievish living on the common road?
This I must do, or know not what to do:
Yet this I will not do, do how I can—
I rather will subject me to the malice
Of a diverted blood and bloody brother.
  Adam. But do not so: I have five hundred crowns,
The thrifty hire I saved under your father,
40 Which I did store to be my foster-nurse
When service should in my old limbs lie lame,
And unregarded age in corners thrown.
Take that, and He that doth the ravens feed,
Yea providently caters for the sparrow,
Be comfort to my age...[*he gives him a bag*] Here is
    the gold;
All this I give you. Let me be your servant.
Though I look old, yet I am strong and lusty;
For in my youth I never did apply
Hot and rebellious liquors in my blood,
50 Nor did not with unbashful forehead woo
The means of weakness and debility.
Therefore my age is as a lusty winter,
Frosty, but kindly: let me go with you,
I'll do the service of a younger man
In all your business and necessities.

Orlando. O good old man, how well in thee appears
The constant service of the antique world,
When service sweat for duty, not for meed!
Thou art not for the fashion of these times,
Where none will sweat but for promotion,   60
And having that do choke their service up
Even with the having—it is not so with thee...
But, poor old man, thou prun'st a rotten tree,
That cannot so much as a blossom yield,
In lieu of all thy pains and husbandry.
But come thy ways, we'll go along together,
And ere we have thy youthful wages spent,
We'll light upon some settled low content.
  Adam. Master, go on, and I will follow thee
To the last gasp with truth and loyalty.   70
From seventeen years till now almost fourscore
Here lived I, but now live here no more.
At seventeen years many their fortunes seek,
But at fourscore it is too late a week.
Yet fortune cannot recompense me better
Than to die well, and not my master's debtor.

> [*they leave the orchard*

[2.4.]   *A clearing in the outskirts of the forest*

ROSALIND (as GANYMEDE) *clad as a boy in forester's
dress, and* CELIA (as ALIENA) *clad as a shepherdess,
together with* TOUCHSTONE, *approach slowly and fling
themselves upon the ground under a tree*

  Rosalind. O Jupiter! how weary are my spirits!
  Touchstone. I care not for my spirits, if my legs were
not weary.
  Rosalind. I could find in my heart to disgrace my
man's apparel, and to cry like a woman: but I must

comfort the weaker vessel, as doublet-and-hose ought to
show itself courageous to petticoat: therefore courage,
good Aliena!

Celia. I pray you, bear with me, I cannot go no
10 further.

Touchstone. For my part, I had rather bear with you
than bear you: yet I should bear no cross if I did bear
you, for I think you have no money in your purse.

Rosalind. Well, this is the forest of Arden!

Touchstone. Ay, now am I in Arden, the more fool I.
When I was at home I was in a better place, but travellers
must be content.

Rosalind.   Ay,
Be so, good Touchstone...

    CORIN *and* SILVIUS *draw near*

       Look you, who comes here—
20 A young man and an old in solemn talk.

Corin. That is the way to make her scorn you still.

Silvius. O Corin, that thou knew'st how I do love her!

Corin. I partly guess: for I have loved ere now.

Silvius. No, Corin, being old, thou canst not guess,
Though in thy youth thou wast as true a lover
As ever sighed upon a midnight pillow:
But if thy love were ever like to mine—
As sure I think did never man love so—
How many actions most ridiculous
30 Hast thou been drawn to by thy fantasy?

Corin. Into a thousand that I have forgotten.

Silvius. O, thou didst then ne'er love so heartily.
If thou remembrest not the slightest folly
That ever love did make thee run into,
Thou hast not loved....
Or if thou hast not sat as I do now,
Wearing thy hearer in thy mistress' praise,

Thou hast not loved....
Or if thou hast not broke from company
Abruptly, as my passion now makes me,   40
Thou hast not loved....
O Phebe, Phebe, Phebe!

[he buries his face in his hands and runs into the forest
Rosalind. Alas, poor shepherd! searching of thy wound,
I have by hard adventure found mine own.

Touchstone. And I mine: I remember, when I was in
love I broke my sword upon a stone, and bid him take
that for coming a-night to Jane Smile, and I remember
the kissing of her batler and the cow's dugs that her
pretty chopt hands had milked; and I remember the
wooing of a peascod instead of her, from whom I took   50
two cods, and giving her them again, said with weeping
tears, 'Wear these for my sake'...We that are true lovers
run into strange capers; but as all is mortal in nature,
so is all nature in love mortal in folly.

Rosalind. Thou speak'st wiser than thou art ware of.

Touchstone. Nay, I shall ne'er be ware of mine own
wit till I break my shins against it.

Rosalind. Jove, Jove! this shepherd's passion
                    Is much upon my fashion.

Touchstone. And mine—but it grows something stale   60
with me.

Celia. I pray you, one of you question yond man
If he for gold will give us any food,
I faint almost to death.

Touchstone.   Holla; you, clown!

Rosalind. Peace, fool, he's not thy kinsman.

Corin.   Who calls?

Touchstone. Your betters, sir.

Corin.   Else are they very wretched.

Rosalind. Peace, I say...Good even to you, friend.

    Corin. And to you, gentle sir, and to you all.

    Rosalind. I prithee, shepherd, if that love or gold

Can in this desert place buy entertainment,

70 Bring us where we may rest ourselves and feed:

Here's a young maid with travel much oppressed,

And faints for succour.

    Corin.   Fair sir, I pity her,

And wish, for her sake more than for mine own,

My fortunes were more able to relieve her:

But I am shepherd to another man,

And do not shear the fleeces that I graze:

My master is of churlish disposition,

And little recks to find the way to heaven

By doing deeds of hospitality:

80 Besides, his cote, his flocks and bounds of feed

Are now on sale, and at our sheepcote now

By reason of his absence there is nothing

That you will feed on; but what is, come see,

And in my voice most welcome shall you be.

    Rosalind. What is he that shall buy his flock

        and pasture?

    Corin. That young swain that you saw here

        but erewhile,

That little cares for buying any thing.

    Rosalind. I pray thee, if it stand with honesty,

Buy thou the cottage, pasture, and the flock,

90 And thou shalt have to pay for it of us.

    Celia. And we will mend thy wages: I like this place,

And willingly could waste my time in it.

    Corin. Assuredly, the thing is to be sold...

Go with me. If you like upon report

The soil, the profit, and this kind of life,

I will your very faithful feeder be,

And buy it with your gold right suddenly.

               [*he goes; they rise and follow him*

[2. 5.]   *Before the cave of the exiled Duke*

'*AMIENS, JAQUES and others,*' *seated beneath the tree*

Amiens [*sings*]. Under the greenwood tree,
         Who loves to lie with me,
         And turn his merry note
         Unto the sweet bird's throat...
     Come hither, come hither, come hither:
         Here shall he see
         No enemy,
     But winter and rough weather.

Jaques. More, more, I prithee, more.

Amiens. It will make you melancholy, Monsieur 10
Jaques.

Jaques. I thank it...More, I prithee, more. I can
suck melancholy out of a song, as a weasel sucks eggs...
More, I prithee, more.

Amiens. My voice is ragged, I know I cannot please you.

Jaques. I do not desire you to please me, I do desire
you to sing...Come, more, another stanzo: call you 'em
stanzos?

Amiens. What you will, Monsieur Jaques.

Jaques. Nay, I care not for their names, they owe me 20
nothing....Will you sing?

Amiens. More at your request than to please myself.

Jaques. Well then, if ever I thank any man, I'll thank
you: but that they call compliment is like th'encounter
of two dog-apes; and when a man thanks me heartily,
methinks I have given him a penny and he renders me
the beggarly thanks....Come, sing; and you that will
not, hold your tongues.

Amiens. Well, I'll end the song....Sirs, cover the
while—the duke will drink under this tree...He hath 30
been all this day to look you.

     [*Some of the company prepare a meal beneath the tree*

Jaques. And I have been all this day to avoid him...
He is too disputable for my company...I think of as
many matters as he, but I give heaven thanks, and make
no boast of them....Come, warble, come.

They sing 'altogether here'

Who doth ambition shun,
And loves to live i'th' sun...
Seeking the food he eats,
And pleased with what he gets...
40   Come hither, come hither, come hither:
Here shall he see
No enemy,
But winter and rough weather.

Jaques. I'll give you a verse to this note, that I made
yesterday in despite of my invention.

Amiens. And I'll sing it.

Jaques. Thus it goes:

If it do come to pass,
That any man turn ass...
50   Leaving his wealth and ease,
A stubborn will to please,
Ducdame, ducdame, ducdame:
Here shall he see,
Gross fools as he,
An if he will come to me.

Amiens. What's that 'ducdame'?

Jaques. 'Tis a Greek invocation, to call fools into a
circle....I'll go sleep, if I can: if I cannot, I'll rail against
all the first-born of Egypt.

60   *Amiens.* And I'll go seek the duke; his banquet is
prepared.   [*they depart in different directions*

[2.6.] *The clearing in the outskirts of the forest*

ORLANDO *and* ADAM *approach*

Adam. Dear master, I can go no further: O, I die for food....[*he falls*] Here lie I down, and measure out my grave....Farewell, kind master.

Orlando. Why, how now, Adam! no greater heart in thee? Live a little, comfort a little, cheer thyself a little. If this uncouth forest yield any thing savage, I will either be food for it or bring it for food to thee...Thy conceit is nearer death than thy powers....[*he lifts him tenderly and props him against a tree*] For my sake be comfortable—hold death awhile at the arm's end: I will here be 10 with thee presently, and if I bring thee not something to eat, I will give thee leave to die: but if thou diest before I come, thou art a mocker of my labour....[*Adam smiles a little*] Well said! thou look'st cheerly, and I'll be with thee quickly...Yet thou liest in the bleak air....[*he takes him in his arms*] Come, I will bear thee to some shelter—and thou shalt not die for lack of a dinner, if there live any thing in this desert....Cheerly, good Adam!   [*he carries him away*

[2.7.]   *Before the cave of the exiled Duke*

A meal of fruit and wine set out under the tree; the DUKE *and some of his lords reclining thereat*

Duke. I think he be transformed into a beast, For I can no where find him like a man.

First Lord. My lord, he is but even now gone hence, Here was he merry, hearing of a song.

Duke. If he, compact of jars, grow musical, We shall have shortly discord in the spheres: Go, seek him, tell him I would speak with him.

Jaques is seen coming through the trees, a smile upon his face, and shortly behind him AMIENS, who silently takes his seat next to the Duke at the meal when he comes up

    First Lord. He saves my labour by his own approach.
    Duke. Why, how now, monsieur! what a life is this,
10 That your poor friends must woo your company?
What, you look merrily!
    Jaques [breaks into laughter]. A fool, a fool! I met a
      fool i'th' forest,
A motley fool—a miserable world!—
As I do live by food, I met a fool,
Who laid him down and basked him in the sun,
And railed on Lady Fortune in good terms,
In good set terms, and yet a motley fool....
'Good morrow, fool,' quoth I: 'No, sir,' quoth he,
'Call me not fool till heaven hath sent me fortune.'
20 And then he drew a dial from his poke,
And looking on it with lack-lustre eye,
Says very wisely, 'It is ten o'clock:
Thus we may see,' quoth he, 'how the world wags:
'Tis but an hour ago since it was nine,
And after one hour more 'twill be eleven,
And so from hour to hour, we ripe, and ripe,
And then from hour to hour, we rot, and rot—
And thereby hangs a tale.'...When I did hear
The motley fool thus moral on the time,
30 My lungs began to crow like chanticleer,
That fools should be so deep-contemplative;
And I did laugh, sans intermission,
An hour by his dial....O noble fool!
O worthy fool! Motley's the only wear.
    Duke. What fool is this?

Jaques. A worthy fool...one that hath been a courtier,
And says, if ladies be but young and fair,
They have the gift to know it: and in his brain,
Which is as dry as the remainder biscuit
After a voyage, he hath strange places crammed   40
With observation, the which he vents
In mangled forms....O, that I were a fool!
I am ambitious for a motley coat.
  Duke. Thou shalt have one.
  Jaques.   It is my only suit—
Provided that you weed your better judgements
Of all opinion that grows rank in them
That I am wise....I must have liberty
Withal, as large a charter as the wind,
To blow on whom I please, for so fools have:
And they that are most galléd with my folly,   50
They most must laugh: and why, sir, must they so?
The 'why' is plain as way to parish church:
He that a fool doth very wisely hit
Doth very foolishly, although he smart,
Not to seem senseless of the bob: if not,
The wise man's folly is anatomized
Even by the squand'ring glances of the fool....
Invest me in my motley; give me leave
To speak my mind, and I will through and through
Cleanse the foul body of th'infected world,   60
If they will patiently receive my medicine.
  Duke. Fie on thee! I can tell what thou wouldst do.
  Jaques. What, for a counter, would I do but
    good?
  Duke. Most mischievous foul sin, in chiding sin:
For thou thyself hast been a libertine,
As sensual as the brutish sting itself,
And all th'embosséd sores and headed evils,

That thou with licence of free foot hast caught,
Wouldst thou disgorge into the general world.

70   *Jaques.* Why, who cries out on pride,
That can therein tax any private party?
Doth it not flow as hugely as the sea,
†Till that the weary very means do ebb?
What woman in the city do I name,
When that I say the city-woman bears
The cost of princes on unworthy shoulders?
Who can come in and say that I mean her,
When such a one as she such is her neighbour?
Or what is he of basest function,

80   That says his bravery is not on my cost,
Thinking that I mean him, but therein suits
His folly to the mettle of my speech?
There then!—how then? what then? Let me see wherein
My tongue hath wronged him: if it do him right,
Then he hath wronged himself; if he be free,
Why then my taxing like a wild-goose flies,
Unclaimed of any man....But who comes here?

ORLANDO appears before them, with his sword drawn

Orlando. Forbear, and eat no more.
Jaques.   Why, I have eat none yet.
Orlando. Nor shalt not, till necessity be served.

90   *Jaques.* Of what kind should this cock come of?
Duke. Art thou thus boldened, man, by thy distress?
Or else a rude despiser of good manners,
That in civility thou seem'st so empty?

Orlando. You touched my vein at first. The
          thorny point
Of bare distress hath ta'en from me the show
Of smooth civility: yet am I inland bred,
And know some nurture...But forbear, I say,

He dies that touches any of this fruit
Till I and my affairs are answeréd.
   Jaques [*taking up a bunch of raisins*]. An you will 100
not be answered with reason, I must die.
   Duke. What would you have? Your gentleness
      shall force,
More than your force move us to gentleness.
   Orlando. I almost die for food, and let me have it.
   Duke. Sit down and feed, and welcome to our table.
   Orlando. Speak you so gently? Pardon me, I
      pray you—
I thought that all things had been savage here,
And therefore put I on the countenance
Of stern commandment. But whate'er you are
That in this desert inaccessible, 110
Under the shade of melancholy boughs,
Lose and neglect the creeping hours of time;
If ever you have looked on better days;
If ever been where bells have knolled to church;
If ever sat at any good man's feast;
If ever from your eyelids wiped a tear,
And know what 'tis to pity and be pitied,
Let gentleness my strong enforcement be:
In the which hope I blush, and hide my sword.
   Duke. True is it that we have seen better days, 120
And have with holy bell been knolled to church,
And sat at good men's feasts, and wiped our eyes
Of drops that sacred pity hath engendred:
And therefore sit you down in gentleness,
And take upon command what help we have
That to your wanting may be ministred.
   Orlando. Then but forbear your food a little while,
Whiles, like a doe, I go to find my fawn,
And give it food....There is an old poor man,

130 Who after me hath many a weary step
    Limped in pure love: till he be first sufficed,
    Oppressed with two weak evils, age and hunger,
    I will not touch a bit.
    Duke.   Go find him out,
    And we will nothing waste till you return
    Orlando. I thank ye, and be blessed for your
        good comfort!   *[he goes*
    Duke. Thou seest we are not all alone unhappy:
    This wide and universal theatre
    Presents more woeful pageants than the scene
    Wherein we play in.
    Jaques.   All the world's a stage,
140 And all the men and women merely players;
    They have their exits and their entrances,
    And one man in his time plays many parts,
    His acts being seven ages....At first the infant,
    Mewling and puking in the nurse's arms:
    Then the whining school-boy, with his satchel
    And shining morning face, creeping like snail
    Unwillingly to school: and then the lover,
    Sighing like furnace, with a woeful ballad
    Made to his mistress' eyebrow: then a soldier,
150 Full of strange oaths and bearded like the pard,
    Jealous in honour, sudden and quick in quarrel,
    Seeking the bubble reputation
    Even in the cannon's mouth: and then the justice,
    In fair round belly with good capon lined,
    With eyes severe and beard of formal cut,
    Full of wise saws and modern instances,
    And so he plays his part....The sixth age shifts
    Into the lean and slippered pantaloon,
    With spectacles on nose and pouch on side,
160 His youthful hose, well saved, a world too wide

For his shrunk shank, and his big manly voice,
Turning again toward childish treble, pipes
And whistles in his sound....Last scene of all,
That ends this strange eventful history,
Is second childishness, and mere oblivion,
Sans teeth, sans eyes, sans taste, sans every thing.

ORLANDO returns with ADAM in his arms

Duke. Welcome...Set down your venerable burden,
And let him feed.
Orlando. I thank you most for him.
Adam.   Sô had you need,
I scarce can speak to thank you for myself.   170
Duke. Welcome, fall to: I will not trouble you
As yet to question you about your fortunes:
Give us some music, and good cousin, sing.

Amiens sings.

> Blow, blow, thou winter wind,
>   Thou art not so unkind
>   As man's ingratitude:
>   Thy tooth is not so keen,
>   Because thou art not seen,
>   Although thy breath be rude....
> Hey-ho, sing hey-ho, unto the green holly,   180
> Most friendship is feigning; most loving mere folly:
>   Then hey-ho, the holly,
>   This life is most jolly.
>
> Freeze, freeze, thou bitter sky,
>   That dost not bite so nigh
>   As benefits forgot:
>   Though thou the waters warp,
>   Thy sting is not so sharp
>   As friend remembred not....

190   Hey-ho, sing hey-ho, unto the green holly,
              Most friendship is feigning; most loving mere folly:
                  Then hey-ho, the holly,
                      This life is most jolly.

       Duke. If that you were the good Sir Rowland's son,
As you have whispered faithfully you were,
And as mine eye doth his effigies witness
Most truly limned and living in your face,
Be truly welcome hither: I am the duke
That loved your father. The residue of your fortune,
200 Go to my cave and tell me....Good old man,
Thou art right welcome as thy master is:
Support him by the arm....Give me your hand,
And let me all your fortunes understand.
                                        [*they enter the cave*

[3. 1.]   *A room in the palace of Duke Frederick*

Enter Duke FREDERICK, *lords, and* OLIVER, *guarded
                    by attendants*

       Duke Frederick. Not see him since? Sir, sir, that
           cannot be:
But were I not the better part made mercy,
I should not seek an absent argument
Of my revenge, thou present: but look to it,
Find out thy brother wheresoe'er he is—
Seek him with candle; bring him dead or living
Within this twelvemonth, or turn thou no more
To seek a living in our territory....
Thy lands and all things that thou dost call thine
10 Worth seizure do we seize into our hands,
Till thou canst quit thee by thy brother's mouth
Of what we think against thee.
       Oliver. O, that your highness knew my heart in this!
I never loved my brother in my life.

Duke Frederick. More villain thou....Well, push him
    out of doors,
And let my officers of such a nature
Make an extent upon his house and lands:
Do this expediently and turn him going.   *[they go*

[3. 2.] *The clearing in the outskirts of the forest, near
    the sheepcote*

ORLANDO *with a paper, which he fixes to
    the trunk of a tree*

Orlando. Hang there, my verse, in witness of my love,
    And thou, thrice-crownéd queen of night, survey
With thy chaste eye, from thy pale sphere above,
    Thy huntress' name that my full life doth sway....
O Rosalind! these trees shall be my books,
    And in their barks my thoughts I'll character,
That every eye which in this forest looks
    Shall see thy virtue witnessed every where....
Run, run, Orlando, carve on every tree
The fair, the chaste and unexpressive she.   10
        [he passes on

CORIN *and* TOUCHSTONE *come up*

Corin. And how like you this shepherd's life, Master
Touchstone?

Touchstone. Truly, shepherd, in respect of itself, it is
a good life; but in respect that it is a shepherd's life, it
is naught. In respect that it is solitary, I like it very well;
but in respect that it is private, it is a very vile life. Now
in respect it is in the fields, it pleaseth me well; but in
respect it is not in the court, it is tedious. As it is a spare
life, look you, it fits my humour well; but as there is no
more plenty in it, it goes much against my stomach. 20
Hast any philosophy in thee, shepherd?

Corin. No more, but that I know the more one

sickens, the worse at ease he is; and that he that wants
money, means and content is without three good friends;
that the property of rain is to wet and fire to burn;
that good pasture makes fat sheep; and that a great cause
of the night, is lack of the sun; that he that hath learned
no wit by nature nor art may complain of good breeding
or comes of a very dull kindred.

30 *Touchstone.* Such a one is a natural philosopher...
Wast ever in court, shepherd?

Corin. No, truly.

Touchstone. Then thou art damned.

Corin. Nay, I hope—

Touchstone. Truly thou art damned, like an ill-
roasted egg all on one side.

Corin. For not being at court? Your reason.

Touchstone. Why, if thou never wast at court, thou
never saw'st good manners; if thou never saw'st good
40 manners, then thy manners must be wicked, and wicked-
ness is sin, and sin is damnation...Thou art in a parlous
state, shepherd.

Corin. Not a whit, Touchstone. Those that are good
manners at the court are as ridiculous in the country,
as the behaviour of the country is most mockable at the
court. You told me you salute not at the court, but you
kiss your hands; that courtesy would be uncleanly, if
courtiers were shepherds.

Touchstone. Instance, briefly; come, instance.

50 *Corin.* Why, we are still handling our ewes, and their
fells you know are greasy.

Touchstone. Why, do not your courtier's hands sweat?
and is not the grease of a mutton as wholesome as the
sweat of a man? Shallow, shallow: a better instance, I
say: come.

Corin. Besides, our hands are hard.

Touchstone. Your lips will feel them the sooner. Shallow, again: a more sounder instance, come.

Corin. And they are often tarred over with the surgery of our sheep; and would you have us kiss tar? The 60 courtier's hands are perfumed with civet.

Touchstone. Most shallow man! thou worms-meat, in respect of a good piece of flesh indeed! Learn of the wise, and perpend: civet is of a baser birth than tar, the very uncleanly flux of a cat. Mend the instance, shepherd.

Corin. You have too courtly a wit for me, I'll rest.

Touchstone. Wilt thou rest damned? God help thee, shallow man! God make incision in thee! thou art raw.   70

Corin. Sir, I am a true labourer. I earn that I eat, get that I wear, owe no man hate, envy no man's happiness, glad of other men's good, content with my harm; and the greatest of my pride is to see my ewes graze and my lambs suck.

Touchstone. That is another simple sin in you, to bring the ewes and the rams together, and to offer to get your living by the copulation of cattle—to be bawd to a bell-wether, and to betray a she-lamb of a twelvemonth to a crookcd-pated, old, cuckoldly ram, out of all reason- 80 able match. If thou beest not damned for this, the devil himself will have no shepherds—I cannot see else how thou shouldst 'scape.

Corin. Here comes young Master Ganymede, my new mistress's brother.

ROSALIND, unwitting of their presence, comes up, sees ORLANDO'S paper on the tree and, plucking it down, begins to read it

Rosalind. 'From the east to western Ind,
          No jewel is like Rosalind.

Her worth, being mounted on the wind,
Through all the world bears Rosalind.
90   All the pictures fairest lined
Are but black to Rosalind....
Let no face be kept in mind
But the fair of Rosalind.'

Touchstone [*taps her on the arm with his bauble*]. I'll rhyme you so eight years together, dinners, and suppers, and sleeping-hours excepted: it is the right butter-women's rank to market.

Rosalind. Out, fool!

Touchstone. For a taste....

100   If a hart do lack a hind,
Let him seek out Rosalind:
If the cat will after kind,
So be sure will Rosalind:
Winter garments must be lined,
So must slender Rosalind.
They that reap must sheaf and bind,
Then to cart with Rosalind.
Sweetest nut hath sourest rind,
Such a nut is Rosalind.
110   He that sweetest rose will find,
Must find love's prick and Rosalind.

This is the very false gallop of verses. Why do you infect yourself with them?

Rosalind. Peace, you dull fool! I found them on a tree.

Touchstone. Truly, the tree yields bad fruit.

Rosalind. I'll graff it with you, and then I shall graff it with a medlar: then it will be the earliest fruit i'th' country: for you'll be rotten ere you be half ripe, and 120 that's the right virtue of the medlar.

Touchstone. You have said: but whether wisely or no, let the forest judge.

CELIA draws near, likewise reading a paper

Rosalind. Peace!
Here comes my sister, reading. Stand aside.
                     [they hide behind a tree
  Celia. 'Why should this a desert be?
      For it is unpeopled? No;
      Tongues I'll hang on every tree,
        That shall civil sayings show.
      Some, how brief the life of man
        Runs his erring pilgrimage,   130
      That the stretching of a span
        Buckles in his sum of age;
      Some, of violated vows
        'Twixt the souls of friend and friend:
      But upon the fairest boughs,
        Or at every sentence end,
      Will I Rosalinda write,
        Teaching all that read to know
      The quintessence of every sprite
        Heaven would in little show.   140
      Therefore Heaven Nature charged,
        That one body should be filled
      With all graces wide-enlarged:
        Nature presently distilled
      Helen's cheek, but not her heart,
        Cleopatra's majesty,
      Atalanta's better part,
        Sad Lucretia's modesty....
      Thus Rosalind of many parts
        By heavenly synod was devised,   150
      Of many faces, eyes, and hearts,
        To have the touches dearest prized....
  Heaven would that she these gifts should have,
  And I to live and die her slave.'

Rosalind. O most gentle pulpiter, what tedious homily of love have you wearied your parishioners withal, and never cried, 'Have patience, good people!'

Celia [*starts and turns, dropping the paper*]. How now, back-friends! Shepherd, go off a little....Go with 160 him, sirrah.

Touchstone. Come, shepherd, let us make an honourable retreat—though not with bag and baggage, yet with scrip and scrippage.

[*Touchstone picks up the verses and departs with Corin*

Celia. Didst thou hear these verses?

Rosalind. O, yes, I heard them all, and more too, for some of them had in them more feet than the verses would bear.

Celia. That's no matter: the feet might bear the verses.

Rosalind. Ay, but the feet were lame, and could not 170 bear themselves without the verse, and therefore stood lamely in the verse.

Celia. But didst thou hear without wondering how thy name should be hanged and carved upon these trees?

Rosalind. I was seven of the nine days out of the wonder before you came; for look here what I found on a palm-tree...I was never so be-rhymed since Pythagoras' time, that I was an Irish rat, which I can hardly remember.

Celia. Trow you who hath done this?

180 *Rosalind.* Is it a man?

Celia. And a chain that you once wore about his neck! Change you colour?

Rosalind. I prithee, who?

Celia. O Lord, Lord! it is a hard matter for friends to meet; but mountains may be removed with earthquakes and so encounter.

Rosalind. Nay, but who is it?

Celia. Is it possible?

Rosalind. Nay, I prithee now with most petitionary vehemence, tell me who it is.   190

Celia. O wonderful, wonderful, and most wonderful wonderful! and yet again wonderful, and after that out of all whooping!

Rosalind. Good my complexion! dost thou think, though I am caparisoned like a man, I have a doublet-and-hose in my disposition? One inch of delay more is a South-sea of discovery....I prithee, tell me who is it quickly, and speak apace: I would thou couldst stammer, that thou mightst pour this concealed man out of thy mouth, as wine comes out of a narrow-mouthed bottle; 200 either too much at once, or none at all. I prithee take the cork out of thy mouth that I may drink thy tidings.

Celia. So you may put a man in your belly.

Rosalind. Is he of God's making? What manner of man? Is his head worth a hat? or his chin worth a beard?

Celia. Nay, he hath but a little beard.

Rosalind. Why, God will send more, if the man will be thankful: let me stay the growth of his beard, if thou delay me not the knowledge of his chin.

Celia. It is young Orlando, that tripped up the 210 wrestler's heels, and your heart, both in an instant.

Rosalind. Nay, but the devil take mocking; speak sad brow and true maid.

Celia. I'faith, coz, 'tis he.

Rosalind. Orlando?

Celia. Orlando.

Rosalind. Alas the day, what shall I do with my doublet and hose? What did he when thou saw'st him? What said he? How looked he? Wherein went he? What makes he here? Did he ask for me? Where remains he? 220 How parted he with thee? and when shalt thou see him again? Answer me in one word.

Celia. You must borrow me Gargantua's mouth first: 'tis a word too great for any mouth of this age's size. To say ay and no to these particulars is more than to answer in a catechism.

Rosalind. But doth he know that I am in this forest and in man's apparel? Looks he as freshly as he did the day he wrestled?

230 *Celia.* It is as easy to count atomies as to resolve the propositions of a lover: but take a taste of my finding him, and relish it with good observance. I found him under a tree, like a dropped acorn.

Rosalind. It may well be called Jove's tree, when it drops such fruit.

Celia. Give me audience, good madam.

Rosalind. Proceed.

Celia. There lay he, stretched along, like a wounded knight.

240 *Rosalind.* Though it be pity to see such a sight, it well becomes the ground.

Celia. Cry 'holla' to thy tongue, I prithee; it curvets unseasonably....He was furnished like a hunter.

Rosalind. O ominous! he comes to kill my heart.

Celia. I would sing my song without a burden—thou bring'st me out of tune.

Rosalind. Do you not know I am a woman? when I think, I must speak...Sweet, say on.

ORLANDO *and* JAQUES *are seen coming through the trees*

Celia. You bring me out....Soft! comes he not here?

250 *Rosalind.* 'Tis he—slink by, and note him.

[*Celia and Rosalind steal behind a tree, within earshot*

Jaques. I thank you for your company—but, good faith,
    I had as lief have been myself alone.

Orlando. And so had I: but yet, for fashion sake,
I thank you too for your society.

Jaques. God buy you, let's meet as little as we can.

Orlando. I do desire we may be better strangers.

Jaques. I pray you, mar no more trees with writing
love-songs in their barks.

Orlando. I pray you, mar no mo of my verses with
reading them ill-favouredly.   260

Jaques. Rosalind is your love's name?

Orlando. Yes, just.

Jaques. I do not like her name.

Orlando. There was no thought of pleasing you when
she was christened.

Jaques. What stature is she of?

Orlando. Just as high as my heart.

Jaques. You are full of pretty answers: have you not
been acquainted with goldsmiths' wives, and conned
them out of rings?   270

Orlando. Not so; but I answer you right painted cloth,
from whence you have studied your questions.

Jaques. You have a nimble wit; I think 'twas made
of Atalanta's heels....Will you sit down with me? and
we two will rail against our mistress the world, and all
our misery.

Orlando. I will chide no breather in the world but
myself, against whom I know most faults.

Jaques. The worst fault you have is to be in love.

Orlando. 'Tis a fault I will not change for your   280
best virtue...I am weary of you.

Jaques. By my troth, I was seeking for a fool when
I found you.

Orlando. He is drowned in the brook—look but in,
and you shall see him.

Jaques. There I shall see mine own figure.

Orlando. Which I take to be either a fool or a cipher.

Jaques. I'll tarry no longer with you. Farewell, good
290 Signior Love.   [*he bows*

Orlando. I am glad of your departure: [*he bows likewise*] adieu, good Monsieur Melancholy.

[*Jaques departs*

(*Rosalind.* I will speak to him like a saucy lackey, and .under that habit play the knave with him.

[*calls*] Do you hear, forester?

Orlando [*turns*]. Very well. What would you?

Rosalind. I pray you, what is't o'clock?

Orlando. You should ask me what time o'day: there's no clock in the forest.

300 *Rosalind.* Then there is no true lover in the forest, else sighing every minute and groaning every hour would detect the lazy foot of Time as well as a clock.

Orlando. And why not the swift foot of Time? had not that been as proper?

Rosalind. By no means, sir: Time travels in divers paces with divers persons...I'll tell you who Time ambles withal, who Time trots withal, who Time gallops withal, and who he stands still withal.

Orlando. I prithee, who doth he trot withal?

310 *Rosalind.* Marry, he trots hard with a young maid between the contract of her marriage and the day it is solemnized: if the interim be but a se'nnight, Time's pace is so hard that it seems the length of seven year.

Orlando. Who ambles Time withal?

Rosalind. With a priest that lacks Latin, and a rich man that hath not the gout: for the one sleeps easily because he cannot study, and the other lives merrily because he feels no pain: the one lacking the burden of

lean and wasteful learning; the other knowing no burden 320
of heavy tedious penury....These Time ambles withal.

Orlando. Who doth he gallop withal?

Rosalind. With a thief to the gallows: for though he
go as softly as foot can fall, he thinks himself too soon
there.

Orlando. Who stays it still withal?

Rosalind. With lawyers in the vacation: for they sleep
between term and term, and then they perceive not how
Time moves.

Orlando. Where dwell you, pretty youth?   330

Rosalind. With this shepherdess, my sister; here in the
skirts of the forest, like fringe upon a petticoat.

Orlando. Are you native of this place?

Rosalind. As the cony that you see dwell where she
is kindled.

Orlando. Your accent is something finer than you
could purchase in so removed a dwelling.

Rosalind. I have been told so of many: but indeed an
old religious uncle of mine taught me to speak, who was
in his youth an inland man—one that knew courtship 340
too well, for there he fell in love....I have heard him
read many lectures against it, and I thank God I am
not a woman, to be touched with so many giddy offences
as he hath generally taxed their whole sex withal.

Orlando. Can you remember any of the principal evils
that he laid to the charge of women?

Rosalind. There were none principal, they were all
like one another as halfpenny are, every one fault
seeming monstrous till his fellow-fault came to match it.

Orlando. I prithee, recount some of them.   350

Rosalind. No: I will not cast away my physic but on
those that are sick....There is a man haunts the forest,
that abuses our young plants with carving 'Rosalind' on

their barks; hangs odes upon hawthorns and elegies on brambles; all, forsooth, deifying the name of Rosalind: if I could meet that fancy-monger, I would give him some good counsel, for he seems to have the quotidian of love upon him.

Orlando. I am he that is so love-shaked. I pray you,
360 tell me your remedy.

Rosalind. There is none of my uncle's marks upon you: he taught me how to know a man in love; in which cage of rushes I am sure you are not prisoner.

Orlando. What were his marks?

Rosalind. A lean cheek, which you have not: a blue eye and sunken, which you have not: an unquestionable spirit, which you have not: a beard neglected, which you have not...but I pardon you for that, for simply your having in beard is a younger brother's revenue.
370 Then your hose should be ungartered, your bonnet unbanded, your sleeve unbuttoned, your shoe untied, and every thing about you demonstrating a careless desolation: but you are no such man; you are rather point-device in your accoutrements, as loving yourself than seeming the lover of any other.

Orlando. Fair youth, I would I could make thee believe I love.

Rosalind. Me believe it! you may as soon make her that you love believe it, which I warrant she is apter to
380 do than to confess she does: that is one of the points in the which women still give the lie to their consciences.... But, in good sooth, are you he that hangs the verses on the trees, wherein Rosalind is so admired?

Orlando. I swear to thee, youth, by the white hand of Rosalind, I am that he, that unfortunate he.

Rosalind. But are you so much in love as your rhymes speak?

Orlando. Neither rhyme nor reason can express how much.

Rosalind. Love is merely a madness, and I tell you 390 deserves as well a dark house and a whip as madmen do: and the reason why they are not so punished and cured is, that the lunacy is so ordinary that the whippers are in love too...Yet I profess curing it by counsel.

Orlando. Did you ever cure any so?

Rosalind. Yes, one, and in this manner. He was to imagine me his love, his mistress; and I set him every day to woo me: at which time would I, being but a moonish youth, grieve, be effeminate, changeable, long- 400 ing and liking, proud, fantastical, apish, shallow, inconstant, full of tears, full of smiles; for every passion something, and for no passion truly any thing, as boys and women are for the most part cattle of this colour: would now like him, now loathe him; then entertain him, then forswear him; now weep for him, then spit at him; that I drave my suitor from his mad humour of love to a living humour of madness—which was, to forswear the full stream of the world and to live in a nook merely monastic...And thus I cured him, and this way 410 will I take upon me to wash your liver as clean as a sound sheep's heart, that there shall not be one spot of love in't.

Orlando. I would not be cured, youth.

Rosalind. I would cure you, if you would but call me Rosalind, and come every day to my cote, and woo me.

Orlando. Now, by the faith of my love, I will...Tell me where it is.

Rosalind. Go with me to it, and I'll show it you: and by the way you shall tell me where in the forest you 420 live...Will you go?

Orlando. With all my heart, good youth.

Rosalind. Nay, you must call me Rosalind...Come, sister, will you go?   [*they go*

Some days pass

[3. 3.]   *The clearing near the sheepcote (as before)*

TOUCHSTONE *and* AUDREY *approach;* JAQUES *following at a little distance*

Touchstone. Come apace, good Audrey. I will fetch up your goats, Audrey...And how, Audrey? am I the man yet? Doth my simple feature content you?

Audrey. Your features, Lord warrant us! what features?

Touchstone. I am here with thee and thy goats, as the most capricious poet, honest Ovid, was among the Goths.

(*Jaques.* O knowledge ill-inhabited! worse than Jove in a thatched house!

10 *Touchstone.* When a man's verses cannot be understood, nor a man's good wit seconded with the forward child, understanding, it strikes a man more dead than a great reckoning in a little room....Truly, I would the gods had made thee poetical.

Audrey. I do not know what 'poetical' is: is it honest in deed and word? is it a true thing?

Touchstone. No, truly; for the truest poetry is the most feigning; and lovers are given to poetry; and what they swear in poetry it may be said as lovers they do feign.

20 *Audrey.* Do you wish then that the gods had made me poetical?

Touchstone. I do, truly: for thou swear'st to me thou art honest; now, if thou wert a poet, I might have some hope thou didst feign.

Audrey. Would you not have me honest?

Touchstone. No, truly, unless thou wert hard-favoured: for honesty coupled to beauty is to have honey a sauce to sugar.

(*Jaques.* A material fool!

Audrey. Well, I am not fair, and therefore I pray the 30 gods make me honest.

Touchstone. Truly, and to cast away honesty upon a foul slut were to put good meat into an unclean dish.

Audrey. I am not a slut, though I thank the gods I am foul.

Touchstone. Well, praised be the gods for thy foulness! sluttishness may come hereafter....But be it as it may be, I will marry thee: and to that end, I have been with Sir Oliver Martext the vicar of the next village, who 40 hath promised to meet me in this place of the forest and to couple us.

(*Jaques.* I would fain see this meeting.

Audrey. Well, the gods give us joy!

Touchstone. Amen....A man may, if he were of a fearful heart, stagger in this attempt; for here we have no temple but the wood, no assembly but horn-beasts. But what though? Courage! As horns are odious, they are necessary. It is said, 'many a man knows no end of his goods'. Right! Many a man has good horns, and 50 knows no end of them. Well, that is the dowry of hi wife; 'tis none of his own getting...Horns? Even so. Poor men alone? No, no, the noblest deer hath them as huge as the rascal...Is the single man therefore blessed? No, as a walled town is more worthier than a village, so is the forehead of a married man more honourable than the bare brow of a bachelor: and by how much defence is better than no skill, by so much is a horn more precious than to want....

SIR OLIVER MARTEXT comes up

60 Here comes Sir Oliver...Sir Oliver Martext, you are
well met. Will you dispatch us here under this tree, or
shall we go with you to your chapel?

Sir Oliver Martext. Is there none here to give the
woman?

Touchstone. I will not take her on gift of any man.

Sir Oliver Martext. Truly, she must be given, or the
marriage is not lawful.

Jaques [*comes forward, doffing his hat*]. Proceed, proceed; I'll give her.

70 *Touchstone.* Good even, good Master What-ye-call't:
how do you, sir? You are very well met: God'ild you
for your last company—I am very glad to see you—even
a toy in hand here, sir...Nay, pray be covered.

Jaques. Will you be married, motley?

Touchstone. As the ox hath his bow, sir, the horse his
curb, and the falcon her bells, so man hath his desires;
and as pigeons bill, so wedlock would be nibbling.

Jaques. And will you, being a man of your breeding,
be married under a bush like a beggar? Get you to
80 church, and have a good priest that can tell you what
marriage is—this fellow will but join you together as they
join wainscot, then one of you will prove a shrunk
panel, and like green timber warp, warp.

(*Touchstone.* I am not in the mind but I were better to
be married of him than of another, for he is not like
to marry me well...and not being well married, it will
be a good excuse for me hereafter to leave my wife.

Jaques. Go thou with me, and let me counsel thee.

Touchstone. Come, sweet Audrey,

90 We must be married, or we must live in bawdry...
Farewell, good Master Oliver: not— [*sings and dances*

     O sweet Oliver,
     O brave Oliver,
    Leave me not behind thee:

but—

     Wind away,
     Begone, I say,
    I will not to wedding with thee.
    [he dances off, Jaques and Audrey following
Sir Oliver Martext. 'Tis no matter; ne'er a fantastical
knave of them all shall flout me out of my calling. 100
          [he goes

[3. 4.] *ROSALIND and CELIA come along the path from
  the cottage; Rosalind drops upon a bank*

Rosalind. Never talk to me, I will weep.

Celia. Do, I prithee—but yet have the grace to con-
sider that tears do not become a man.

Rosalind. But have I not cause to weep?

Celia. As good cause as one would desire, therefore
weep.

Rosalind. His very hair is of the dissembling colour.

Celia. Something browner than Judas's: marry, his
kisses are Judas's own children.

Rosalind. I'faith, his hair is of a good colour. 10

Celia. An excellent colour: your chestnut was ever the
only colour.

Rosalind. And his kissing is as full of sanctity as the
touch of holy bread.

Celia. He hath bought a pair of cast lips of Diana:
a nun of winter's sisterhood kisses not more religiously,
the very ice of chastity is in them.

Rosalind. But why did he swear he would come this
morning, and comes not?

Celia. Nay, certainly, there is no truth in him. 20

Rosalind. Do you think so?

Celia. Yes, I think he is not a pick-purse nor a horse-stealer, but for his verity in love I do think him as concave as a covered goblet or a worm-eaten nut.

Rosalind. Not true in love?

Celia. Yes, when he is in—but I think he is not in.

Rosalind. You have heard him swear downright he was.

Celia. 'Was' is not 'is': besides, the oath of a lover
30 is no stronger than the word of a tapster, they are both the confirmer of false reckonings. He attends here in the forest on the duke your father.

Rosalind. I met the duke yesterday and had much question with him: he asked me of what parentage I was; I told him, of as good as he—so he laughed and let me go....But what talk we of fathers, when there is such a man as Orlando?

Celia. O, that's a brave man! he writes brave verses, speaks brave words, swears brave oaths and breaks
40 them bravely, quite traverse, athwart the heart of his lover—as a puny tilter, that spurs his horse but on one side, breaks his staff like a noble goose; but all's brave that youth mounts and folly guides....Who comes here?

CORIN *draws near and accosts them*

Corin. Mistress and master, you have oft inquired
After the shepherd that complained of love,
Who you saw sitting by me on the turf,
Praising the proud disdainful shepherdess
That was his mistress.

Celia.   Well: and what of him?

Corin. If you will see a pageant truly played,
50 Between the pale complexion of true love
And the red glow of scorn and proud disdain,

Go hence a little and I shall conduct you,
If you will mark it.
  Rosalind.   O, come, let us remove.
The sight of lovers feedeth those in love:
Bring us to this sight, and you shall say
I'll prove a busy actor in their play.   *[they go*

[3. 5.]   *Another part of the forest*
     PHEBE, followed by SILVIUS who entreats her

  Silvius [kneels]. Sweet Phebe, do not scorn me, do
    not, Phebe:
Say that you love me not, but say not so
In bitterness...The common executioner,
Whose heart th'accustomed sight of death makes hard,
Falls not the axe upon the humbled neck
But first begs pardon: will you sterner be
Than he that dies and lives by bloody drops?

  ROSALIND, CELIA, and CORIN come up behind, unseen

  Phebe. I would not be thy executioner.
I fly thee, for I would not injure thee...
Thou tell'st me there is murder in mine eye—   10
'Tis pretty, sure, and very probable,
That eyes, that are the frail'st and softest things,
Who shut their coward gates on atomies,
Should be called tyrants, butchers, murderers!
Now I do frown on thee with all my heart,
And if mine eyes can wound, now let them kill thee;
Now counterfeit to swoon, why now fall down,
Or if thou canst not, O for shame, for shame,
Lie not, to say mine eyes are murderers!
Now show the wound mine eye hath made in thee.   20
Scratch thee but with a pin, and there remains
Some scar of it: lean but upon a rush,

The cicatrice and capable impressure
Thy palm some moment keeps: but now mine eyes,
Which I have darted at thee, hurt thee not,
Nor, I am sure, there is no force in eyes
That can do hurt.
    Silvius.   O dear Phebe,
If ever—as that ever may be near—
You meet in some fresh cheek the power of fancy,
30 Then shall you know the wounds invisible
That love's keen arrows make.
    Phebe.   But till that time
Come not thou near me: and when that time comes,
Afflict me with thy mocks, pity me not,
As till that time I shall not pity thee.
    Rosalind [*advancing*]. And why, I pray you? Who
           might be your mother,
That you insult, exult, and all at once,
Over the wretched? What though you have no beauty—
As, by my faith, I see no more in you
Than without candle may go dark to bed—
40 Must you be therefore proud and pitiless?
Why, what means this? Why do you look on me?
I see no more in you than in the ordinary
Of nature's sale-work! 'Od's my little life,
I think she means to tangle my eyes too:
No, faith, proud mistress, hope not after it.
'Tis not your inky brows, your black silk hair,
Your bugle eyeballs, nor your cheek of cream,
That can entame my spirits to your worship...
You foolish shepherd, wherefore do you follow her,
50 Like foggy south, puffing with wind and rain?
You are a thousand times a properer man
Than she a woman: 'tis such fools as you
That makes the world full of ill-favoured children:

'Tis not her glass, but you, that flatters her,
And out of you she sees herself more proper
Than any of her lineaments can show her...
But, mistress, know yourself—down on your knees,
And thank heaven, fasting, for a good man's love;
              [*Phebe kneels to Rosalind*
For I must tell you friendly in your ear,
Sell when you can—you are not for all markets: 60
Cry the man mercy, love him, take his offer.
Foul is most foul, being foul to be a scoffer....
So take her to thee, shepherd—fare you well.
   Phebe. Sweet youth, I pray you chide a year together.
I had rather hear you chide than this man woo.
   Rosalind [*to Phebe*]. He's fallen in love with your
foulness, [*to Silvius*] and she'll fall in love with my
anger. If it be so, as fast as she answers thee with
frowning looks, I'll sauce her with bitter words...[*to
Phebe*] Why look you so upon me?   70
   Phebe. For no ill will I bear you.
   Rosalind. I pray you, do not fall in love with me,
For I am falser than vows made in wine:
Besides, I like you not...If you will know my house,
'Tis at the tuft of olives here hard by...
Will you go, sister? Shepherd, ply her hard...
Come, sister...Shepherdess, look on him better,
And be not proud—though all the world could see,
None could be so abused in sight as he....
Come, to our flock.   80
         [*she stalks away followed by Celia and Corin*
   Phebe [*gazing after them*]. Dead Shepherd, now I
     find thy saw of might,
'Who ever loved that loved not at first sight?'
   Silvius. Sweet Phebe—
   Phebe.   Ha! what say'st thou, Silvius?

Silvius. Sweet Phebe, pity me.

Phebe. Why, I am sorry for thee, gentle Silvius.

Silvius. Wherever sorrow is, relief would be:
If you do sorrow at my grief in love,
By giving love your sorrow and my grief
Were both extermined.

90   *Phebe.* Thou hast my love—is not that neighbourly?

Silvius. I would have you.

Phebe.   Why, that were covetousness...
Silvius, the time was that I hated thee,
And yet it is not that I bear thee love;
But since that thou canst talk of love so well,
Thy company, which erst was irksome to me,
I will endure; and I'll employ thee too:
But do not look for further recompense
Than thine own gladness that thou art employed.

Silvius. So holy and so perfect is my love,

100 And I in such a poverty of grace,
That I shall think it a most plenteous crop
To glean the broken ears after the man
That the main harvest reaps: loose now and then
A scattered smile, and that I'll live upon.

Phebe. Know'st thou the youth that spoke to me
        erewhile?

Silvius. Not very well, but I have met him oft,
And he hath bought the cottage and the bounds
That the old carlot once was master of.

Phebe. Think not I love him, though I ask for him.

110 'Tis but a peevish boy—yet he talks well—
But what care I for words?—yet words do well,
When he, that speaks them pleases those that hear:
It is a pretty youth—not very pretty—
But, sure, he's proud—and yet his pride becomes him:
He'll make a proper man: the best thing in him

Is his complexion; and faster than his tongue
Did make offence, his eye did heal it up:
He is not very tall—yet for his years he's tall:
His leg is but so so—and yet 'tis well:
There was a pretty redness in his lip,   120
A little riper and more lusty red
Than that mixed in his cheek; 'twas just the difference
Betwixt the constant red and mingled damask....
There be some women, Silvius, had they marked him
In parcels as I did, would have gone near
To fall in love with him: but, for my part,
I love him not, nor hate him not; and yet
I have more cause to hate him than to love him,
For what had he to do to chide at me?
He said mine eyes were black and my hair black,   130
And, now I am remembered, scorn'd at me:
I marvel why I answered not again:
But that's all one; omittance is no quittance:
I'll write to him a very taunting letter,
And thou shalt bear it—wilt thou, Silvius?
  Silvius. Phebe, with all my heart.
  Phebe.   I'll write it straight;
The matter's in my head and in my heart.
I will be bitter with him and passing short:
Go with me, Silvius.   [*they go*

[4. 1.]   *The clearing near the sheepcote*

Enter ROSALIND, CELIA, *and* JAQUES

  Jaques. I prithee, pretty youth, let me be better
acquainted with thee.
  Rosalind. They say you are a melancholy fellow.
  Jaques. I am so: I do love it better than laughing.
  Rosalind. Those that are in extremity of either are

abominable fellows, and betray themselves to every
modern censure worse than drunkards.

Jaques. Why, 'tis good to be sad and say nothing.

Rosalind. Why then, 'tis good to be a post.

10 *Jaques.* I have neither the scholar's melancholy,
which is emulation; nor the musician's, which is fantastical; nor the courtier's, which is proud; nor the
soldier's, which is ambitious; nor the lawyer's, which is
politic; nor the lady's, which is nice; nor the lover's,
which is all these: but it is a melancholy of mine own,
compounded of many simples, extracted from many
objects, and indeed the sundry contemplation of my
travels, in which my often rumination wraps me in a
most humorous sadness.

20 *Rosalind.* A traveller! By my faith, you have great
reason to be sad: I fear you have sold your own lands
to see other men's; then, to have seen much, and to have
nothing, is to have rich eyes and poor hands.

Jaques. Yes, I have gained my experience.

ORLANDO *draws near*

Rosalind. And your experience makes you sad: I had
rather have a fool to make me merry than experience
to make me sad—and to travel for it too!

Orlando. Good day, and happiness, dear Rosalind!

[*she takes no heed of him*

Jaques. Nay then, God buy you, an you talk in blank

30 verse.   [*he turns from them*

Rosalind. Farewell, Monsieur Traveller: look you
lisp and wear strange suits; disable all the benefits of
your own country; be out of love with your nativity,
and almost chide God for making you that countenance
you are; or I will scarce think you have swam in a
gondola....[*Jaques passes out of earshot; she sits*] Why,

how now, Orlando! where have you been all this while?
You a lover! An you serve me such another trick, never
come in my sight more.

Orlando. My fair Rosalind, I come within an hour of 40
my promise.

Rosalind. Break an hour's promise in love? He that
will divide a minute into a thousand parts, and break
but a part of the thousandth part of a minute in the
affairs of love, it may be said of him that Cupid hath
clapped him o'th' shoulder, but I'll warrant him heart-
whole.

Orlando. Pardon me, dear Rosalind.

Rosalind. Nay, an you be so tardy come no more in
my sight, I had as lief be wooed of a snail.   50

Orlando. Of a snail?

Rosalind. Ay, of a snail; for though he comes slowly,
he carries his house on his head; a better jointure, I
think, than you make a woman: besides, he brings his
destiny with him.

Orlando. What's that?   [*he sits beside her*

Rosalind. Why, horns; which such as you are fain to
be beholding to your wives for: but he comes armed in
his fortune, and prevents the slander of his wife.

Orlando. Virtue is no horn-maker...[*musing*] and my 60
Rosalind is virtuous.

Rosalind. And I am your Rosalind.

[*she puts her arm about his neck*

Celia. It pleases him to call you so; but he hath a
Rosalind of a better leer than you.

Rosalind. Come, woo me, woo me; for now I am in a
holiday humour, and like enough to consent...What
would you say to me now, an I were your very very
Rosalind?

Orlando. I would kiss before I spoke.

70 *Rosalind.* Nay, you were better speak first, and when
you were gravelled for lack of matter, you might take
occasion to kiss: very good orators, when they are out,
they will spit, and for lovers, lacking (God warr'nt us!)
matter, the cleanliest shift is to kiss.

Orlando. How if the kiss be denied?

Rosalind. Then she puts you to entreaty and there
begins new matter.

Orlando. Who could be out, being before his beloved
mistress?

80 *Rosalind.* Marry, that should you if I were your mistress, or I should think my honesty ranker than my wit.

Orlando. What, of my suit?

Rosalind. Not out of your apparel, and yet out of your
suit...Am not I your Rosalind?

Orlando. I take some joy to say you are, because I
would be talking of her.

Rosalind. Well, in her person, I say I will not have
you.

Orlando. Then in mine own person, I die.

90 *Rosalind.* No, faith, die by attorney: the poor world
is almost six thousand years old, and in all this time
there was not any man died in his own person, videlicet,
in a love-cause: Troilus had his brains dashed out with
a Grecian club, yet he did what he could to die before,
and he is one of the patterns of love: Leander, he would
have lived many a fair year, though Hero had turned
nun, if it had not been for a hot midsummer night; for,
good youth, he went but forth to wash him in the
Hellespont and being taken with the cramp was drowned,
100 and the foolish chroniclers of that age found it was
'Hero of Sestos.'....But these are all lies. Men have
died from time to time, and worms have eaten them,
but not for love.

Orlando. I would not have my right Rosalind of this mind, for I protest her frown might kill me.

Rosalind. By this hand, it will not kill a fly...[*draws closer to him*] But come, now I will be your Rosalind in a more coming-on disposition; and ask me what you will, I will grant it.

Orlando. Then love me, Rosalind.   110

Rosalind. Yes, faith will I, Fridays and Saturdays and all.

Orlando. And wilt thou have me?

Rosalind. Ay, and twenty such.

Orlando. What sayest thou?

Rosalind. Are you not good?

Orlando. I hope so.

Rosalind. Why then, can one desire too much of a good thing? [*she rises*] Come, sister, you shall be the priest and marry us....Give me your hand, Orlando... 120 What do you say, sister?

Orlando. Pray thee, marry us.

Celia. I cannot say the words.

Rosalind. You must begin, 'Will you, Orlando'—

Celia. Go to...Will you, Orlando, have to wife this Rosalind?

Orlando. I will.

Rosalind. Ay, but when?

Orlando. Why now, as fast as she can marry us.

Rosalind. Then you must say, 'I take thee, Rosalind, 130 for wife.'

Orlando. I take thee, Rosalind, for wife.

Rosalind. I might ask you for your commission, but I do take thee, Orlando, for my husband...There's a girl goes before the priest, and certainly a woman's thought runs before her actions.

Orlando. So do all thoughts, they are winged.

Rosalind. Now tell me how long you would have her after you have possessed her.

140 *Orlando.* For ever and a day.

Rosalind. Say 'a day' without the 'ever'...No, no, Orlando, men are April when they woo, December when they wed; maids are May when they are maids, but the sky changes when they are wives...I will be more jealous of thee than a Barbary cock-pigeon over his hen, more clamorous than a parrot against rain, more new-fangled than an ape, more giddy in my desires than a monkey: I will weep for nothing, like Diana in the fountain, and I will do that when you are disposed 150 to be merry; I will laugh like a hyen, and that when thou art inclined to sleep.

Orlando. But will my Rosalind do so?

Rosalind. By my life, she will do as I do.

Orlando. O, but she is wise.

Rosalind. Or else she could not have the wit to do this: the wiser, the waywarder: make the doors upon a woman's wit, and it will out at the casement; shut that, and 'twill out at the key-hole; stop that, 'twill fly with the smoke out at the chimney.

160 *Orlando.* A man that had a wife with such a wit, he might say 'Wit, whither wilt?'

Rosalind. Nay, you might keep that check for it, till you met your wife's wit going to your neighbour's bed.

Orlando. And what wit could wit have to excuse that?

Rosalind. Marry, to say she came to seek you there... You shall never take her without her answer, unless you take her without her tongue: O, that woman that cannot make her fault her husband's occasion, let her 170 never nurse her child herself, for she will breed it like a fool.

Orlando. For these two hours, Rosalind, I will leave thee.

Rosalind. Alas, dear love, I cannot lack thee two hours!

Orlando. I must attend the duke at dinner. By two o'clock I will be with thee again.

Rosalind. Ay, go your ways, go your ways; I knew what you would prove, my friends told me as much, and I thought no less: that flattering tongue of yours won me: 'tis but one cast away, and so, come death.... 180 Two o'clock is your hour?

Orlando. Ay, sweet Rosalind.

Rosalind. By my troth, and in good earnest, and so God mend me, and by all pretty oaths that are not dangerous, if you break one jot of your promise, or come one minute behind your hour, I will think you the most pathetical break-promise, and the most hollow lover, and the most unworthy of her you call Rosalind, that may be chosen out of the gross band of the unfaithful: therefore beware my censure, and keep your 190 promise.

Orlando. With no less religion than if thou wert indeed my Rosalind: so adieu.

Rosalind. Well, Time is the old justice that examines all such offenders, and let Time try: adieu!   [*he goes*

Celia. You have simply misused our sex in your love-prate: we must have your doublet and hose plucked over your head, and show the world what the bird hath done to her own nest.

Rosalind. O coz, coz, coz...my pretty little coz, that 200 thou didst know how many fathom deep I am in love! But it cannot be sounded; my affection hath an unknown bottom, like the bay of Portugal.

Celia. Or rather, bottomless—that as fast as you pour affection in, it runs out.

Rosalind. No, that same wicked bastard of Venus, that
was begot of thought, conceived of spleen, and born of
madness—that blind rascally boy that abuses every one's
eyes because his own are out—let him be judge how
210 deep I am in love...I'll tell thee, Aliena, I cannot be out
of the sight of Orlando: I'll go find a shadow and sigh
till he come.

Celia. And I'll sleep.   [*they go*

[4. 2.] *Before the cave of the exiled Duke. A noise as
of huntsmen approaching. Presently* AMIENS *and other
lords appear, dressed as foresters, with* JAQUES *in their
midst to whom they are telling of their morning's sport*

Jaques. Which is he that killed the deer?
A lord. Sir, it was I.
Jaques. Let's present him to the duke, like a Roman
conqueror. And it would do well to set the deer's horns
upon his head, for a branch of victory...Have you no
song, forester, for this purpose?
Amiens. Yes, sir.
Jaques. Sing it: 'tis no matter how it be in tune, so it
make noise enough.

*He that killed the deer is first clad in horns and skin,
and then raised aloft by the company, who 'sing him home,'
Amiens leading and the rest joining in chorus*

The Song

10   What shall he have that killed the deer?
His leather skin and horns to wear:
Then sing him home—the rest shall bear
This burden...
Take thou no scorn to wear the horn,
It was a crest ere thou wast born,

Thy father's father wore it,
And thy father bore it,
The horn, the horn, the lusty horn,
Is not a thing to laugh to scorn.

*They march thrice around the tree, repeating the burthen
again and again; then they turn into the Duke's cave*

[4. 3.]   *The clearing near the sheepcote*

ROSALIND *and* CELIA *return*

Rosalind. How say you now? Is it not past two
o'clock? and here much Orlando!

Celia. I warrant you, with pure love and troubled
brain, he hath ta'en his bow and arrows, and is gone
forth to sleep...Look, who comes here.

SILVIUS *approaches*

Silvius. My errand is to you, fair youth
My gentle Phebe bid me give you this:

                    [*he gives Rosalind a letter*
I know not the contents, but as I guess
By the stern brow and waspish action
Which she did use as she was writing of it,   10
It bears an angry tenour: pardon me,
I am but as a guiltless messenger.

Rosalind. Patience herself would startle at this letter,
And play the swaggerer—bear this, bear all:
She says I am not fair, that I lack manners,
She calls me proud, and that she could not love me
Were man as rare as phœnix: 'od's my will!
Her love is not the hare that I do hunt.
Why writes she so to me? Well, shepherd, well, ·
This is a letter of your own device.   20

Silvius. No, I protest, I know not the contents—
Phebe did write it.

Rosalind.   Come, come, you are a fool,
And turned into the extremity of love.
I saw her hand—she has a leathern hand,
A freestone-coloured hand: I verily did think
That her old gloves were on, but 'twas her hands:
She has a huswife's hand—but that's no matter:
I say she never did invent this letter,
This is a man's invention, and his hand.

30 *Silvius.* Sure, it is hers.

Rosalind. Why, 'tis a boisterous and a cruel style,
A style for challengers; why, she defies me,
Like Turk to Christian: women's gentle brain
Could not drop forth such giant-rude invention,
Such Ethiop words, blacker in their effect
Than in their countenance...Will you hear the letter?

Silvius. So please you, for I never heard it yet;
Yet heard too much of Phebe's cruelty.

Rosalind. She Phebes me: mark how the tyrant writes.

40 [*reads*]   'Art thou god to shepherd turned,
                    That a maiden's heart hath burned?'
Can a woman rail thus?

Silvius. Call you this railing?

Rosalind. 'Why, thy godhead laid apart,
                    Warr'st thou with a woman's heart?'
Did you ever hear such railing?
                    'Whiles the eye of man did woo me,
                    That could do no vengeance to me.'
Meaning me a beast.

50   'If the scorn of your bright eyne
                    Have power to raise such love in mine,
                    Alack, in me what strange effect
                    Would they work in mild aspéct?
                    Whiles you chid me I did love,
                    How then might your prayers move?

He that brings this love to thee
Little knows this love in me:
And by him seal up thy mind,
Whether that thy youth and kind
Will the faithful offer take   60
Of me and all that I can make,
Or else by him my love deny,
And then I'll study how to die.'

Silvius. Call you this chiding?

Celia. Alas, poor shepherd!

Rosalind. Do you pity him? no, he deserves no pity...
Wilt thou love such a woman? What, to make thee an
instrument and play false strains upon thee! not to be
endured! Well, go your way to her (for I see love hath
made thee a tame snake) and say this to her: that if she   70
love me, I charge her to love thee: if she will not, I will
never have her, unless thou entreat for her....If you be
a true lover, hence, and not a word; for here comes more
company.   [*he goes*

OLIVER comes up hastily by another path

Oliver. Good morrow, fair ones: pray you, if
      you know,
Where in the purlieus of this forest stands
A sheepcote fenced about with olive-trees?

Celia. West of this place, down in the
      neighbour bottom—
The rank of osiers by the murmuring stream
Left on your right hand brings you to the place   80
But at this hour the house doth keep itself,
There's none within.

Oliver. If that an eye may profit by a tongue,
Then should I know you by description—
Such garments and such years: 'The boy is fair,

Of female favour, and bestows himself
†Like a ripe forester: the woman low,
And browner than her brother.'...Are not you
The owner of the house I did inquire for?

90   *Celia.* It is no boast, being asked, to say we are.
    Oliver. Orlando doth commend him to you both,
And to that youth he calls his Rosalind
He sends this bloody napkin; are you he?
    Rosalind. I am: what must we understand by this?
    Oliver. Some of my shame, if you will know of me
What man I am, and how, and why, and where
This handkercher was stained.
    Celia.   I pray you, tell it.
    Oliver. When last the young Orlando parted from you
He left a promise to return again
100 Within an hour, and pacing through the forest,
Chewing the food of sweet and bitter fancy,
Lo, what befel! he threw his eye aside,
And mark what object did present itself!
Under an oak, whose boughs were mossed with age
And high top bald with dry antiquity,
A wretched ragged man, o'ergrown with hair,
Lay sleeping on his back: about his neck
A green and gilded snake had wreathed itself,
Who with her head nimble in threats approached
110 The opening of his mouth; but suddenly
Seeing Orlando, it unlinked itself,
And with indented glides did slip away
Into a bush: under which bush's shade
A lioness, with udders all drawn dry,
Lay couching, head on ground, with catlike watch,
When that the sleeping man should stir; for 'tis
The royal disposition of that beast
To prey on nothing that doth seem as dead:

This seen, Orlando did approach the man,
And found it was his brother, his elder brother.   120
  Celia. O, I have heard him speak of that same brother,
And he did render him the most unnatural
That lived 'mongst men.
  Oliver.   And well he might so do,
For well I know he was unnatural.
  Rosalind. But, to Orlando: did he leave him there,
Food to the sucked and hungry lioness?
  Oliver. Twice did he turn his back and purposed so:
But kindness, nobler ever than revenge,
And nature, stronger than his just occasion,
Made him give battle to the lioness,   130
Who quickly fell before him: in which hurtling
From miserable slumber I awaked.
  Celia. Are you his brother?
  Rosalind.   Was't you he rescued?
  Celia. Was't you that did so oft contrive to kill him?
  Oliver. 'Twas I; but 'tis not I: I do not shame
To tell you what I was, since my conversion
So sweetly tastes, being the thing I am.
  Rosalind. But, for the bloody napkin?—
  Oliver.   By and by...
When from the first to last betwixt us two
Tears our recountments had most kindly bathed,   140
As how I came into that desert place....
In brief, he led me to the gentle duke,
Who gave me fresh array and entertainment,
Committing me unto my brother's love,
Who led me instantly unto his cave,
There stripped himself, and here upon his arm
The lioness had torn some flesh away,
Which all this while had bled; and now he fainted,
And cried, in fainting, upon Rosalind....

150 Brief, I recovered him, bound up his wound,
And after some small space being strong at heart,
He sent me hither, stranger as I am,
To tell this story, that you might excuse
His broken promise, and to give this napkin,
Dyed in his blood, unto the shepherd youth
That he in sport doth call his Rosalind.

                                    [*Rosalind faints*
    Celia. Why, how now, Ganymede! sweet Gany-
        mede!
    Oliver. Many will swoon when they do look on blood.
    Celia. There is more in it...Cousin, Ganymede!
160 *Oliver.* Look, he recovers.
    Rosalind.   I would I were at home.
    Celia. We'll lead you thither...
I pray you, will you take him by the arm?
    Oliver. Be of good cheer, youth: you a man!
You lack a man's heart.
    Rosalind.   I do so, I confess it...
Ah, sirrah, a body would think this was well counterfeited. I pray you, tell your brother how well I
counterfeited....Heigh-ho!
    Oliver. This was not counterfeit, there is too great
testimony in your complexion that it was a passion of
170 earnest.
    Rosalind. Counterfeit, I assure you.
    Oliver. Well then, take a good heart, and counterfeit
to be a man.
    Rosalind. So I do: but, i'faith, I should have been a
woman by right.
    Celia. Come, you look paler and paler; pray you,
draw homewards...Good sir, go with us.
    Oliver. That will I: for I must bear answer back
How you excuse my brother, Rosalind.

Rosalind. I shall devise something: but, I pray you commend my counterfeiting to him...Will you go?

[*they descend towards the cottage*

[5. 1.] TOUCHSTONE *and* AUDREY *come through the trees*

Touchstone. We shall find a time, Audrey—patience, gentle Audrey.

Audrey. Faith, the priest was good enough, for all the old gentleman's saying.

Touchstone. A most wicked Sir Oliver, Audrey, a most vile Martext....But, Audrey, there is a youth here in the forest lays claim to you.

Audrey. Ay, I know who 'tis; he hath no interest in me in the world: here comes the man you mean.

WILLIAM *enters the clearing*

Touchstone. It is meat and drink to me to see a clown. 10 By my troth, we that have good wits have much to answer for; we shall be flouting; we cannot hold.

William. Good ev'n, Audrey.

Audrey. God ye good ev'n, William.

William. And good ev'n to you, sir.

Touchstone [*with mock-dignity*]. Good ev'n, gentle friend. Cover thy head, cover thy head; nay, prithee, be covered....How old are you, friend?

William. Five-and-twenty, sir.

Touchstone. A ripe age...Is thy name, William? 20

William. William, sir.

Touchstone. A fair name...Wast born i'th' forest here?

William. Ay sir, I thank God.

Touchstone. 'Thank God'; a good answer...Art rich?

William. Faith sir, so so.

Touchstone. 'So so' is good, very good, very excellent good: and yet it is not, it is but so so...Art thou wise?

30 *William.* Ay sir, I have a pretty wit.

Touchstone. Why, thou say'st well....I do now remember a saying: 'The fool doth think he is wise, but the wise man knows himself to be a fool'...[*By this William's mouth is wide open with amazement*] The heathen philosopher, when he had a desire to eat a grape, would op'en his lips when he put it into his mouth, meaning thereby that grapes were made to eat and lips to open....You do love this maid?

William. I do, sir.

40 *Touchstone.* Give me your hand...Art thou learned?

William. No, sir.

Touchstone. Then learn this of me—to have, is to have; for it is a figure in rhetoric that drink, being poured out of a cup into a glass, by filling the one doth empty the other; for all your writers do consent that ipse is he: now, you are not ipse, for I am he.

William. Which he, sir?

Touchstone. He, sir, that must marry this woman... Therefore, you clown, abandon (which is in the vulgar

50 'leave') the society (which in the boorish is 'company') of this female (which in the common is 'woman'); which together is, 'abandon the society of this female,' or, clown, thou perishest; or, to thy better understanding, diest; or, to wit, I kill thee, make thee away, translate thy life into death, thy liberty into bondage: I will deal in poison with thee, or in bastinado, or in steel; I will bandy with thee in faction; I will o'er-run thee with policy; I will kill thee a hundred and fifty ways—therefore tremble and depart.

60 *Audrey.* Do, good William.

William. God rest you merry, sir. [*he goes*

CORIN appears and calls

Corin. Our master and mistress seek you: come, away, away.

Touchstone. Trip, Audrey, trip, Audrey—I attend, I attend.   [*they run off towards the cottage*

A night passes

[5. 2.]   OLIVER *and* ORLANDO (*his arm in a scarf*)
seated on a bank

Orlando. Is't possible that on so little acquaintance you should like her? that but seeing you should love her? and loving woo? and, wooing, she should grant? and will you persever to enjoy her?

Oliver. Neither call the giddiness of it in question, the poverty of her, the small acquaintance, my sudden wooing, nor her sudden consenting; but say with me, I love Aliena; say with her that she loves me; consent with both that we may enjoy each other: it shall be to your good; for my father's house and all the revenue 10 that was old Sir Rowland's will I estate upon you, and here live and die a shepherd.

ROSALIND is seen coming in the distance

Orlando. You have my consent....Let your wedding be to-morrow: thither will I invite the duke and all's contented followers...Go you and prepare Aliena; for look you, here comes my Rosalind.

Rosalind. God save you, brother.

Oliver. And you, fair sister.   [*he goes*

Rosalind. O, my dear Orlando, how it grieves me to see thee wear thy heart in a scarf.   20

Orlando. It is my arm.

Rosalind. I thought thy heart had been wounded with the claws of a lion.

Orlando. Wounded it is, but with the eyes of a lady.

Rosalind. Did your brother tell you how I counterfeited to swoon, when he showed me your handkercher?

Orlando. Ay, and greater wonders than that.

Rosalind. O, I know where you are: nay, 'tis true:
there was never any thing so sudden but the fight of
30 two rams, and Cæsar's thrasonical brag of 'I came, saw,
and overcame': for your brother and my sister no sooner
met but they looked; no sooner looked but they loved;
no sooner loved but they sighed; no sooner sighed but
they asked one another the reason; no sooner knew the
reason but they sought the remedy: and in these degrees
have they made a pair of stairs to marriage, which they
will climb incontinent, or else be incontinent before
marriage: they are in the very wrath of love, and they
will together; clubs cannot part them.

40 *Orlando.* They shall be married to-morrow; and I will
bid the duke to the nuptial....But, O, how bitter a thing
it is to look into happiness through another man's eyes!
By so much the more shall I to-morrow be at the height
of heart-heaviness, by how much I shall think my brother
happy in having what he wishes for.

Rosalind. Why then, to-morrow I cannot serve your
turn for Rosalind?

Orlando. I can live no longer by thinking.

Rosalind. I will weary you then no longer with idle
50 talking....Know of me then, for now I speak to some
purpose, that I know you are a gentleman of good conceit: I speak not this that you should bear a good opinion
of my knowledge, insomuch I say I know you are;
neither do I labour for a greater esteem than may in
some little measure draw a belief from you, to do yourself good and not to grace me....Believe then, if you
please, that I can do strange things: I have, since I was

three year old, conversed with a magician, most profound in his art, and yet not damnable....If you do love
Rosalind so near the heart as your gesture cries it out, 60
when your brother marries Aliena, shall you marry her.
I know into what straits of fortune she is driven, and
it is not impossible to me, if it appear not inconvenient
to you, to set her before your eyes to morrow, human
as she is, and without any danger.

Orlando. Speak'st thou in sober meanings?

Rosalind. By my life I do, which I tender dearly,
though I say I am a magician...Therefore, put you in
your best array, bid your friends; for if you will be
married to-morrow, you shall; and to Rosalind, if you 70
will.

SILVIUS and PHEBE draw near

Look, here comes a lover of mine and a lover of hers.

Phebe. Youth, you have done me much ungentleness,
To show the letter that I writ to you.

Rosalind. I care not if I have: it is my study
To seem despiteful and ungentle to you:
You are there followed by a faithful shepherd—
Look upon him, love him; he worships you.

Phebe. Good shepherd, tell this youth what 'tis to
love.

Silvius. It is to be all made of sighs and tears, 80
And so am I for Phebe.

Phebe. And I for Ganymede.

Orlando. And I for Rosalind.

Rosalind. And I for no woman.

Silvius. It is to be all made of faith and service,
And so am I for Phebe.

Phebe. And I for Ganymede.

Orlando. And I for Rosalind.

Rosalind. And I for no woman.

90 *Silvius.* It is to be all made of fantasy,
All made of passion, and all made of wishes,
All adoration, duty and observance,
All humbleness, all patience, and impatience,
All purity, all trial, all obedience;
And so am I for Phebe.

Phebe. And so am I for Ganymede.

Orlando. And so am I for Rosalind.

Rosalind. And so am I for no woman.

Phebe [to Rosalind]. If this be so, why blame you me
to love you?

100 *Silvius [to Phebe].* If this be so, why blame you me
to love you?

Orlando. If this be so, why blame you me to love you?

Rosalind. Who do you speak to, 'Why blame you me
to love you?'

Orlando. To her that is not here, nor doth not hear.

Rosalind. Pray you no more of this, 'tis like the howling
of Irish wolves against the Moon...[*to Silvius*] I will
help you, if I can...[*to Phebe*] I would love you, if I
could...To-morrow meet me all together...[*to Phebe*]
I will marry you, if ever I marry woman, and I'll be
married to-morrow...[*to Orlando*] I will satisfy you, if
110 ever I satisfied man, and you shall be married to-
morrow...[*to Silvius*] I will content you, if what
pleases you contents you, and you shall be married to-
morrow...[*to Orlando*] As you love Rosalind, meet.
[*to Silvius*] As you love Phebe, meet. And as I love
no woman, I'll meet....So, fare you well; I have left
you commands.

Silvius. I'll not fail, if I live.

Phebe. Nor I.

Orlando. Nor I.   [*they disperse*

[5. 3.]   *Touchstone and Audrey enter the clearing*

Touchstone. To-morrow is the joyful day, Audrey. To-morrow will we be married.

Audrey. I do desire it with all my heart: and I hope it is no dishonest desire to desire to be a woman of the world. Here come two of the banished duke's pages.

Two pages run up

First Page. Well met, honest gentleman.

Touchstone. By my troth, well met...Come, sit, sit, and a song.

Second Page. We are for you: sit i'th' middle.

First Page. Shall we clap into't roundly, without 10 hawking or spitting or saying we are hoarse, which are the only prologues to a bad voice?

Second Page. I'faith i'faith; and both in a tune, like two gipsies on a horse.

Song

It was a lover and his lass,
    With a hey, and a ho, and a hey nonino:
That o'er the green corn-field did pass,
    In spring time, the only pretty ring time,
When birds do sing, hey ding a ding, ding,
Sweet lovers love the spring.   20

Between the acres of the rye,
    With a hey, and a ho, and a hey nonino:
These pretty country folks would lie,
    In spring time, the only pretty ring time,
When birds do sing, hey ding a ding, ding,
Sweet lovers love the spring.

This carol they began that hour,
    With a hey, and a ho, and a hey nonino:
How that life was but a flower,

30   In spring time, the only pretty ring time,
        When birds do sing, hey ding a ding, ding,
        Sweet lovers love the spring.

        And therefore take the present time,
            With a hey, and a ho, and a hey nonino:
        For love is crownéd with the prime,
            In spring time, the only pretty ring time,
        When birds do sing, hey ding a ding, ding,
        Sweet lovers love the spring.

Touchstone. Truly, young gentlemen, though there was
40 no great matter in the ditty, yet the note was very un-
tuneable.

First Page. You are deceived, sir—we kept time, we
lost not our time.

Touchstone. By my troth, yes; I count it but time lost
to hear such a foolish song....God buy you, and God
mend your voices! Come, Audrey.   [*they go*

●   *A night passes*

[5. 4.]   *The clearing near the sheepcote* (*as before*)

*The exiled DUKE, AMIENS, JAQUES, ORLANDO,
OLIVER, and CELIA*

Duke. Dost thou believe, Orlando, that the boy
Can do all this that he hath promiséd?
Orlando. I sometimes do believe, and sometimes do not,
As those that fear they hope, and know they fear.

ROSALIND, SILVIUS, and PHEBE join the company

Rosalind. Patience once more, whiles our compáct
        is urged:
You say, if I bring in your Rosalind,
You will bestow her on Orlando here?

Duke. That would I, had I kingdoms to give
   with her.
Rosalind. And you say you will have her, when I
   bring her?
Orlando. That would I, were I of all kingdoms king.   10
Rosalind. You say you'll marry me, if I be willing?
Phebe. That will I, should I die the hour after.
Rosalind. But if you do refuse to marry me,
You'll give yourself to this most faithful shepherd?
Phebe. So is the bargain.
Rosalind. You say that you'll have Phebe, if she
   will?
Silvius. Though to have her and death were both
   one thing.
Rosalind. I have promised to make all this matter
   even...
Keep you your word, O duke, to give your daughter—
You yours, Orlando, to receive his daughter: 20
Keep your word, Phebe, that you'll marry me,
Or else refusing me, to wed this shepherd:
Keep your word, Silvius, that you'll marry her,
If she refuse me—and from hence I go,
To make these doubts all even.
         [she beckons to Celia and they depart together
 Duke. I do remember in this shepherd-boy
Some lively touches of my daughter's favour. 🌹
 Orlando. My lord, the first time that I ever saw
   him,
Methought he was a brother to your daughter:
But, my good lord, this boy is forest-born,   30
And hath been tutored in the rudiments
Of many desperate studies by his uncle,
Whom he reports to be a great magician,
Obscuréd in the circle of this forest.

Touchstone and Audrey enter the clearing

Jaques. There is, sure, another flood toward, and these couples are coming to the ark. Here comes a pair of very strange beasts, which in all tongues are called fools.

Touchstone. Salutation and greeting to you all!

Jaques. Good my lord, bid him welcome: this is the
40 motley-minded gentleman that I have so often met in the forest: he hath been a courtier, he swears.

Touchstone. If any man doubt that, let him put me to my purgation. I have trod a measure—I have flattered a lady—I have been politic with my friend, smooth with mine enemy—I have undone three tailors—I have had four quarrels, and like to have fought one.

Jaques. And how was that ta'en up?

Touchstone. Faith, we met, and found the quarrel was upon the seventh cause.

50 *Jaques.* How seventh cause? Good my lord, like this fellow.

Duke. I like him very well.

Touchstone. God'ild you, sir, I desire you of the like... I press in here, sir, amongst the rest of the country copulatives, to swear and to forswear, according as marriage binds and blood breaks...[*he waves towards Audrey*] A poor virgin, sir, an ill-favoured thing, sir, but mine own—a poor humour of mine, sir, to take that that no man else will: rich honesty dwells like a
60 miser, sir, in a poor house, as your pearl in your foul oyster.

Duke. By my faith, he is very swift and sententious.

Touchstone. According to the fool's bolt, sir, and such dulcet diseases.

Jaques. But, for the seventh cause. How did you find the quarrel on the seventh cause?

Touchstone. Upon a lie seven times removed...bear your body more seeming, Audrey...as thus, sir: I did dislike the cut of a certain courtier's beard: he sent me word, if I said his beard was not cut well, he was in the mind it was: this is called the Retort Courteous. If I sent him word again 'it was not well cut,' he would send me word, he cut it to please himself: this is called the Quip Modest. If again 'it was not well cut,' he disabled my judgement: this is called the Reply Churlish. If again 'it was not well cut,' he would answer, I spake not true: this is called the Reproof Valiant. If again 'it was not well cut,' he would say, I lie: this is called the Countercheck Quarrelsome: and so to the Lie Circumstantial and the Lie Direct.

Jaques. And how oft did you say his beard was not well cut?

Touchstone. I durst go no further than the Lie Circumstantial: nor he durst not give me the Lie Direct: and so we measured swords and parted.

Jaques. Can you nominate in order now the degrees of the lie?

Touchstone. O sir, we quarrel in print—by the book: as you have books for good manners...I will name you the degrees. The first, the Retort Courteous; the second, the Quip Modest; the third, the Reply Churlish; the fourth, the Reproof Valiant; the fifth, the Countercheck Quarrelsome; the sixth, the Lie with Circumstance; the seventh, the Lie Direct...All these you may avoid, but the Lie Direct; and you may avoid that too, with an If. I knew when seven justices could not take up a quarrel, but when the parties were met themselves, one of them thought but of an If; as, 'If you said so, then I said so': and they shook hands and swore brothers. Your If is the only peace-maker; much virtue in If.

Jaques. Is not this a rare fellow, my lord? he's as good at any thing, and yet a fool!

Duke. He uses his folly like a stalking-horse, and under the presentation of that he shoots his wit.

Enter, as in a masque, persons representing Hymen and his train, together with Rosalind and Celia in their proper habits. 'Still music'

> *Hymen sings*
>
>   Then is there mirth in heaven,
>   When earthly things made even
>   Atone together.
>   Good duke, receive thy daughter,
>   Hymen from heaven brought her,
>   Yea, brought her hither,
>   That thou mightst join her hand with his
>   Whose heart within her bosom is.

Rosalind [to the Duke]. To you I give myself, for I am yours.

[to Orlando] To you I give myself, for I am yours.

Duke. If there be truth in sight, you are my daughter.

Orlando. If there be truth in sight, you are my Rosalind.

Phebe. If sight and shape be true, Why then, my love adieu!

Rosalind. I'll have no father, if you be not he: I'll have no husband, if you be not he: Nor ne'er wed woman, if you be not she.

Hymen. Peace, ho! I bar confusion.
>   'Tis I must make conclusion
>   Of these most strange events:
>   Here's eight that must take hands,
>   To join in Hymen's bands,
>   If truth holds true contents.

You and you no cross shall part:
You and you are heart in heart:
You to his love must accord,   130
Or have a woman to your lord.
You and you are sure together,
As the winter to foul weather.
Whiles a wedlock-hymn we sing,
Feed yourselves with questioning;
That reason wonder may diminish,
How thus we met, and these things finish.

Choric song
Wedding is great Juno's crown,
    O blesséd bond of board and bed:
'Tis Hymen peoples every town,   140
    High wedlock then be honouréd:
Honour, high honour and renown,
To Hymen, god of every town!

Duke. O my dear niece, welcome thou art to me,
Even daughter, welcome, in no less degree.

Phebe [*to Silvius*]. I will not eat my word, now
    thou art mine,
Thy faith my fancy to thee doth combine.

Enter JAQUES DE BOYS

Jaques de Boys. Let me have audience for a word
    or two:
I am the second son of old Sir Rowland,
That bring these tidings to this fair assembly.   150
Duke Frederick, hearing how that every day
Men of great worth resorted to this forest,
Addressed a mighty power, which were on foot,
In his own conduct, purposely to take
His brother here and put him to the sword:
And to the skirts of this wild wood he came;

Where, meeting with an old religious man,
After some question with him, was converted
Both from his enterprise and from the world:
160 His crown bequeathing to his banished brother,
And all their lands restored to them again
That were with him exiled...This to be true,
I do engage my life.

    Duke.   Welcome, young man;
Thou offer'st fairly to thy brothers' wedding:
To one his lands withheld, and to the other
A land itself at large, a potent dukedom.
First, in this forest, let us do those ends
That here were well begun and well begot:
And after, every of this happy number,
170 That have endured shrewd days and nights with us,
Shall share the good of our returnéd fortune,
According to the measure of their states.
Meantime, forget this new-fall'n dignity,
And fall into our rustic revelry...
Play, music! and you brides and bridegrooms all,
With measure heaped in joy, to th' measures fall.

    Jaques. Sir, by your patience...   *[he stays the music*
[to Jaques de Boys]   If I heard you rightly,
The duke hath put on a religious life,
And thrown into neglect the pompous court?
180   *Jaques de Boys.* He hath.

    Jaques. To him will I: out of these convertites
There is much matter to be heard and learned....
[to the Duke] You to your former honour I bequeath,
Your patience and your virtue well deserves it:
[to Orlando] You to a love, that your true faith doth
        merit:
[to Oliver] You to your land, and love, and great allies:
[to Silvius] You to a long and well-deservéd bed:

[*to Touchstone*] And you to wrangling, for thy
    loving voyage
Is but for two months victualled…So to your pleasures,
I am for other than for dancing measures.   190
  Duke. Stay, Jaques, stay.
  Jaques. To see no pastime, I: what you would have
I'll stay to know at your abandoned cave.
                       [*he turns from them*
  Duke. Proceed, proceed: we will begin these rites,
As we do trust they'll end in true delights.
            Music and dance

Epilogue

spoken by Rosalind

It is not the fashion to see the lady the epilogue: but
it is no more unhandsome than to see the lord the
prologue. If it be true that good wine needs no bush,
'tis true that a good play needs no epilogue: yet to good
wine they do use good bushes; and good plays prove
the better by the help of good epilogues...What a case
am I in then, that am neither a good epilogue nor
cannot insinuate with you in the behalf of a good play!
I am not furnished like a beggar, therefore to beg will
10 not become me: my way is to conjure you, and I'll
begin with the women. I charge you, O women, for
the love you bear to men, to like as much of this play
as please you: and I charge you, O men, for the love
you bear to women—as I perceive by your simpering,
none of you hates them—that between you and the
women the play may please. If I were a woman, I
would kiss as many of you as had beards that pleased
me, complexions that liked me, and breaths that I defied
not: and, I am sure, as many as have good beards, or
20 good faces, or sweet breaths, will, for my kind offer,
when I make curtsy, bid me farewell.

GLOSSARY

Note. Where a pun or quibble is intended, the meanings are
distinguished as (*a*) and (*b*)

ABUSED, deceived; 3. 5. 79

ADDRESSED, equipped, prepared;
5. 4. 153

ADVENTURE, accident, chance; 2.
4. 44

ALLOTTERY, assignment of a share
(N.E.D. quotes no other instance); 1. 1. 68

AMAZE, confuse, bewilder; 1. 2.
102

ANATOMIZE, lit. dissect (surg.), lay
open minutely, expose; 1. 1.
146; 2. 7. 56

ASPECT, (*a*) glance, (*b*) the favour-
able or unfavourable influence of
a planet according to the old
astrologers; 4. 3. 53

ATOMIES, motes, specks of dust in
a sunbeam; 3. 2. 230; 3. 5. 13

ATONE, unite, come into unity or
concord; 5. 4. 107

BACK-FRIEND, a pretended or false
friend; here used of a person
who comes upon one from behind
(for the same jest see *Err.* 4. 2.
37); 3. 2. 159

BANDY (IN FACTION), give and
take recriminations; 5. 1. 57

BANQUET, a light repast of fruit
and wine, often served as dessert
after supper; 2. 5. 60

BARBARY COCK-PIGEON, 'a fancy
variety of pigeon, of black or
dun colour originally introduced
from Barbary' (N.E.D. 'barb' 2);
4. 1. 145

BASTINADO, a beating or cudgelling,
esp. upon the soles of the feet;
5. 1. 56

BATLER, a kind of wooden club for
'battling' (v. N.E.D.) or beating
clothes during the process of
washing; 2. 4. 48

BEGGARLY, like a beggar; 2. 5. 27

BESTOW ONESELF, to acquit oneself,
bear oneself (cf. *Two Gent.* 3. 1.
87); 4. 3. 86

BILL, advertisement, proclamation
(cf. *Ado*, 1. 1. 36); 1. 2. 114

BLUE EYE, i.e. with dark circles
round the eye as from sleepless-
ness or weeping; 3. 2. 365

BOB, lit. (i) trick, deception, (ii)
sharp rap or blow with the fist;
and so, by combining the two
meanings, 'taunt, bitter jest,
jibe' (N.E.D.); 2. 7. 55

BONNY. N.E.D. states 'it appears
to have often had the sense: Of
fine size, big (as a good quality),'
and quotes Hooker 'bonny and
strong enough unto any labours';
2. 3. 8

BOTTOM, dell, valley; 4. 3. 78

BOUNDS (OF FEED), 'limits within
which he had the rights of
pasturage' (Aldis Wright). Pre-
sumably these rights were in
respect of the common land; 2.
4. 80; 3. 5. 107

BOW, a yoke for oxen; 3. 3. 75

BREATHED, exercised; 'well breathed' = put into good wind; 1. 2.
207

BREATHER, living being, creature
(cf. *Son.* 81. 12; *Ant.* 3. 3. 24);
3. 2. 277

BUCKLE IN, encompass, limit; 3. 2.
132

BUGLE, i.e. black as bugle (= ornamental tubĕ-shaped bead-work); 3. 5. 47

BUR, (a) prickly seed-vessel, (b) 'a bur in the throat' = anything that produced a choking sensation in the throat (N.E.D. 'bur' 4); 1. 3. 16

BURTHEN, accompaniment to a song, part for the bass; 3. 2. 245

BUSH, lit. 'a branch or bunch of ivy (perhaps as a plant sacred to Bacchus) hung up as a vintner's sign' (N.E.D.), and hence the tavern-sign itself; Ep. 3

BUTCHERY, slaughter-house, shambles; 2. 3. 27

CAGE OF RUSHES. A 'cage' was a lock-up for petty malefactors; 'a cage of rushes' would be a flimsy prison for a 'prizer' like Orlando; possibly, as Hart suggests, there is a side-glance at the rush-ring, commonly used for mock marriages among rustics (cf. All's Well, 2. 2. 24); 3. 2. 363

CAPABLE, either (i) passive, 'receivable,' or (ii) active, 'receptive, retaining'; 3. 5. 23

CAPON, a cock for eating. A 'capon-justice' was a 17th cent. term for a judge or magistrate bribed by gifts of capons (cf. N.E.D. 'capon'); 2. 7. 154

CARLOT, churl, peasant (N.E.D. quotes no other instance); 3. 5. 108

CAROL, orig. 'a ring-dance with song,' hence 'any kind of song sung at times of festival' (cf. M.N.D. 2. 1. 102); 5. 3. 27

CART, 'to cart with.' Bawds and harlots were punished by public exposure and whipping in a cart drawn through the streets (cf. Lear, 4. 6. 165; Shrew, 1. 1. 55); 3. 2. 107

CAST, cast-off, discarded; 3. 4. 15

CHARACTER, engrave; 3. 2. 6

CHOPT, chapped; 2. 4. 49

CICATRICE, lit. 'the scar of a wound,' hence here 'a scar-like mark'; 3. 5. 23

CIVIL, variously interpreted as (i) grave or solemn, and (ii) civilised or refined; 3. 2. 128

CLAP INTO, 'to enter with alacrity and briskness upon anything' (Dr Johnson); 5. 3. 10

CLAP O'TH' SHOULDER, arrest (cf. Err. 4. 2. 37 'shoulder-clapper' = sergeant); 4. 1. 46

CODS, (a) pods, (b) testicles (cf. N.E.D. 'cod' 4); 2. 4. 51

COMBINE, bind (cf. Meas. 4. 3. 144 'I am combined by a sacred vow'); 5. 4. 147

COMFORTABLE, of good comfort, cheerful (cf. Tim. 3. 4. 71); 2. 6. 9

COMPACT OF, composed of. The word 'compact' also carries the meaning of 'tightly packed'; 2. 7. 5

CONCAVE, hollow (the orig. meaning); 3. 4. 23

CONCEIT, (i) fancy, imagination (cf. Ham. 3. 4. 114); 2. 6. 7; (ii) intelligence, mental capacity; 5. 2. 51

CONDUCT, leadership, command (of an army); 5. 4. 154

CONFINES, region, territory. No sense of 'confinement' intended; 2. 1. 24

CONSTANT (of a colour), uniform; 3. 5. 123

CONTRIVER, schemer, plotter; 1. 1. 136

CONVERTITE, a convert to a religious faith or way of life; 5. 4. 181

COPE, orig. 'to come to blows with, encounter in battle or tournament,' and so 'to hold converse or debate with' (cf. *Ham.* 3. 2. 60); 2. 1. 67

COPULATIVE, orig. a grammatical term; Touchstone, of course, means 'one about to be or desirous of being married'; 5. 4. 55

COUNTERCHECK, rebuke or rebuff (in retaliation for another). 'The figure is from the game of chess' (Ald. Wright); 5. 4. 79, 92

COVER, prepare the table, lay the cloth; 2. 5. 29

COVERED GOBLET. Goblets were generally fitted with ornamental covers, which were of course removed when the goblet was in use: a covered goblet was therefore an empty or 'concave' (q.v.) goblet; 3. 4. 24

CROSS, coin (der. from the practice of stamping one side of coins with the figure of a cross: cf. *L.L.L.* 1. 2. 32–33); 2. 4. 12

CURTLE-AXE. 'A much perverted form of the word "cutlass"' (N.E.D.); a heavy sword for cutting or slashing; 1. 3. 117

DAMASK, the colour of the damask rose, i.e. a blush-colour (cf. *Son.* 130. 5); 3. 5. 123

DEFY, reject, disdain; Ep. 18

DEVICE, invention, ingenuity; 1. 1. 156

DIAL. 'The allusion here may be either to a watch, or to a portable journey-ring or small sun-dial' (Halliwell). Aldis Wright compares *Ric. II*, 5. 5. 53–6;

1 *Hen. IV*, 5. 2. 84, both of which passages speak of the 'dial's point,' and therefore refer to watches or clocks; 2. 7. 20

DISABLE, disparage, belittle; 4. 1. 32; 5. 4. 75

DISCOVERY, (*a*) disclosure, (*b*) exploration (v. N.E.D. 'discovery' 3 *b*); 3. 2. 197

DISHONEST, (*a*) discreditable, (*b*) immodest, unchaste; 5. 3. 4

DISLIKE, express aversion to; 5. 4. 69

DISPUTABLE, disputatious; 2. 5. 33

DITTY, 'the words of a song, as distinguished from the music or tune' (N.E.D.); 5. 3. 40

DIVERTED BLOOD, i.e. 'blood diverted from the course of nature' (Dr Johnson). Shakespeare is using technical medical language; the old doctors professed to be able to 'divert' the course of the humours or the blood by means of medicinal appliances (v. N.E.D. 'diversion' 1 *b*); 2. 3. 37

DOG-APE, 'a dog-faced baboon' (Dyce). Aldis Wright quotes Chapman, *Humorous Day's Mirth*: 'So long as the compliments of a gentleman last, he is your complete ape'; 2. 5. 25

DOUBLET-AND-HOSE, the male attire of the period; we should say 'a man's suit'; 2. 4. 7; 3. 2. 195

DROP FORTH, bring forth; 3. 2. 235; 4. 3. 34

DRY BRAIN. 'In the physiology of Shakespeare's time a dry brain accompanied slowness of apprehension and a retentive memory' (Wright, who quotes *Batman vppon Bartholome*: 'He that hath such a braine receiueth slowly the feeling and printing

of thinges: but neverthelesse
when hee hath taken and re-
ceiued them, he keepeth them
long in mind'); 2. 7. 39

EFFIGIES, likeness, portrait; 2. 7.
196

EMBOSSED, swollen, tumid; 2. 7. 67

ENCHANTINGLY, 'as if under the
influence of a charm' (Wright);
1. 1. 157

ENGAGE, pledge; 5. 4. 163

EREWHILE, a little while back; 2. 4.
86; 3. 5. 105

ESTATE, bestow as an estate upon
(cf. *M.N.D.* 1. 1. 98); 5. 2. 11

EXERCISE, 'such exercises as may
become a gentleman,' i.e. the
occupations necessary for the
training of a young gentleman
(cf. *Two Gent.* 1. 3. 30–3); 1. 1.
67

EXPEDIENTLY, expeditiously,
promptly (N.E.D. quotes no
other instance of this sense); 3.
1. 18

EXTENT, seizure of lands in execu-
tion of a writ, sequestration; 3.
1. 17

EYNE, an old form of 'eyes,' rarely
used by the Elizabethans except
for rhyming purposes; 4. 3. 50

FACTION, dissension, factious
quarrel (v. *bandy*); 5. 1. 57

FALSE GALLOP, canter. Touchstone
quibbles (cf. note 3. 2. 96–7);
3. 2. 112

FANCY, love (of a not too serious
kind); 3. 5. 29

FANCY-MONGER, one who deals in
love; Orlando has filled the
forest with advertisements; 3.
2. 356

FANTASY, imagination (cf. *M.N.D.*
5. 1. 7–8); 2. 4. 30; 5. 2. 90

FAVOUR, appearance, face; 4. 3. 86;
5. 4. 27

FEATURES. If the word be taken
in the old-fashioned sense of
'limbs' or 'parts of the body'
(v. N.E.D. 'feature' 2*b*), it will
be seen that Audrey had a touch
of Widow Wadman about her;
3. 3. 4

FEEDER, shepherd or servant; 2.
4. 96

FELL, the hide of an animal with
the wool or hair; 3. 2. 51

FLEET, to while away the time, to
let the time glide away. The
word is connected with 'float'
(v. N.E.D. 'fleet' v.¹ 10*d*); 1. 1.
112

FLUX, (i) continuous stream; 2. 1.
52; (ii) discharge from the
body; 3. 2. 65

FOIL, to throw (in wrestling); 1.
1. 123; 1. 2. 177; 2. 2. 14

FOND TO (with *inf.*), eager to, glad
to (v. N.E.D. 'fond² A 7); 2.
3. 7

FOOL (POOR), i.e. 'poor dear.'
Shakespeare often uses 'fool'
as a term of endearment or pity;
2. 1. 22, 40

FORKED HEADS, i.e. arrows. There
were two sorts of pointed
arrow: one with the points
looking backward and called the
broad-headed or swallow-tail,
the other with the points
stretching forward and called
the fork-headed or barbed. (See
Ascham, *Toxophilus*, ed. Arber,
pp. 135, 136); 2. 1. 24

FREESTONE-COLOURED, i.e. with
the dirty white or grey colour
of limestone; 4. 3. 25

GAMESTER, (*a*) athlete (N.E.D.
quotes from 1601, 'professed

wrestlers, runners and such gamesters at feats of activity'); (b) merry, frolicsome person; 1. 1. 153

GARGANTUA, the name of the voracious giant in Rabelais, who possessed so large a mouth that he swallowed five pilgrims, with their staves, in a salad; 3. 2. 223

GESTURE, bearing, manner; 5. 2. 60

GOD BUY YOU, the Elizabethan half-way house between 'God be with you' and the modern 'good-bye'; 3. 2. 255; 4. 1. 29; 5. 3. 45

GOD'ILD YOU, i.e. God yield you (where 'yield' = reward, repay) —'a common expression of gratitude or goodwill' (N.E.D.), though becoming archaic in the 17th cent.; 3. 3. 71; 5. 4. 53

GRAFF, an archaic variant of 'graft'; 3. 2. 117

GRAVELLED, perplexed, nonplussed (der. from 'gravelled' = run aground); 4. 1. 71

GREEK, in reference to the sb. meaning 'a cunning or wily person; a cheat, sharper, esp. one who cheats at cards' (N.E.D. sb. 4); 2. 5. 57

GROW UPON, (a) increase (or grow up) so as to become more troublesome, (b) take liberties with, presume upon; 1. 1. 81

HARD, with an uneasy pace. Onions quotes Holme's Armory, 1688, 'a Trotting horse, when he sets hard, and goes of an uneasy pace'; 3. 2. 310

HAVING, possession, property; 3. 2. 369

HEADED, i.e. come to a head, like a boil; 2. 7. 67

HEY-HO. 'An utterance apparently of nautical origin, and marking the rhythm of movement in heaving or hauling; often used in the burdens of songs with various emotional expression, according to intonation' (N.E.D.); 2. 7. 180, etc.

HIND, farm-servant; 1. 1. 18

HOLY BREAD, 'the (ordinary leavened) bread which was blessed after the Eucharist and distributed to those who had not communicated...the eulogia of the Greek Church and the French pain bénit' (N.E.D.); 3. 4. 14

HONEST, chaste; 1. 2. 36; 3. 3. 15, 23, 25, 31

HOOP, shout with astonishment (cf. Hen. V, 2. 2. 108); 3. 2. 193

HUMOROUS, moody; 1. 2. 254

HURTLING, noise of an encounter, collision or battle; 4. 3. 131

HYEN, hyena; 4. 1. 150

ILL-FAVOUREDLY, in an ugly fashion; 1. 2. 37

IMPRESSURE, impression (cf. Tw. Nt. 2. 5. 103); 3. 5. 23

INCISION, engrafting. 'In the 17th century,' N.E.D. tells us, 'incision' was 'often erroneously used for "insition," engrafting' ('incision' 5); 3. 2. 69

INCONTINENT, (a) straightway, (b) unchaste; 5. 2. 37

INDIRECT, wrong, unjust; 1. 1. 143

INLAND, belonging to the districts lying near the capital as opposed to the remote or outlying wild parts (v. N.E.D. 'inland' A3, B1b); 2. 7. 96; 3. 2. 340

INSINUATE, ingratiate oneself with (cf. Marlowe, Massacre of Paris, 2. 4. 'Now, Madam, must you insinuate with the King'); Ep. 8

INSTANCE, illustration, example, proof; 2. 7. 156; 3. 2. 49, 54, 58

INSULT, triumph in an insolent fashion; 3. 5. 36

INTENDMENT, intention, project; 1. 1. 126

IRK, distress, pain; 2. 1. 22

JUST, exactly so. An expression of assent; the word 'quite' is often used to-day colloquially in much the same sense; 3. 2. 262

KIND, (i) sex (cf. *M. of V.* 1. 3. 82); 3. 2. 102; (ii) nature, character, inclination; 4. 3. 59

KINDLE, give birth to (generally used of hares and rabbits); 3. 2. 335

KINDNESS, natural instinct; 4. 3. 128

LEER, (a) face, complexion (a poetical word), (b) ogle; 4. 1. 64

LINE, (i) delineate, sketch; 3. 2. 90; (ii) Cf. Cotgrave, 1611: *Ligner*, To line, as a dog (or dog-wolf) a bitch; 3. 2. 104

LITTLE (IN), in miniature (cf. *Ham.* 2. 2. 383 'his picture in little'). But here Shakespeare is referring to man, who is the microcosm or miniature of the universe (v. note); 3. 2. 140

LIVELY, lifelike (cf. *Tim.* 1. 1. 38); 5. 4. 27

LIVER, formerly considered the seat of the passions; 3. 2. 411

LIVING, real, actual (cf. *Oth.* 3. 3. 409 'Give me a living reason she's disloyal'); 3. 2. 408

LOOK, i.e. look for (cf. *M.W.W.* 4. 2. 75 'I will look some linen'); 2. 5. 31

LUSTY, gay, bright (of a colour); 3. 5. 121

MAKE (THE DOOR), shut, close, bar (cf. *Err.* 3. 1. 93); 4. 1. 156

MANAGE, the action and paces to which a horse is trained when broken in; 1. 1. 12

MANNERS, (a) polite behaviour, (b) in the older sense of 'moral character' (cf. *M. of V.* 2. 3. 19 'Though I am daughter to his blood,/I am not to his manners'); 3. 2. 39, 40

MATERIAL, (a) 'stocked with notions' (Johnson; cf. *matter*); (b) gross, carnal (cf. N.E.D. 'material' 4 b); 3. 3. 29

MATTER, topics for discussion or conversation; 2. 1. 68; 4. 1. 71; 5. 4. 182

MEASURE, a solemn dance, 'full of state and ancientry' (*Ado*, 2. 1. 69); 5. 4. 43, 176, 190

MEWL, mew like a cat. Cf. Cotgrave, 1611: '*Miauler*, to mewle, or mew, like a cat.' Because the word has only survived in modern times through Shakespeare's influence, it has come to mean 'whimper like an infant,' but Jaques was deliberately making comparison with cats; 2. 7. 144

MISPRIZE, fail to appreciate; 1. 1. 159

MISUSE, abuse, revile, misrepresent (cf. *Son.* 152. 7); 4. 1. 196

MO, more in number. Formerly 'more' = 'more in quantity' only; 3. 2. 259

MODERN, commonplace, trite; 2. 7. 156; 4. 1. 7

MOONISH, changeable, fickle; 3. 2. 400

MORALIZE, interpret, expound morally or symbolically; 2. 1. 44

MORTAL, (a) subject to death, (b) 'mortal in folly' = mortally foolish; 2. 4. 53, 54

MOTLEY. There were two sorts of fool at this period: the motley fool and the fool in the yellow petticoat. Apparently the motley fool was the superior intellectually, the other type being the 'natural' or idiot. The motley fool's costume consisted of a parti-coloured coat, with bells on the elbows or at the skirts; close hose and breeches, generally with the two legs of a different colour; and a hood decorated with asses' ears or cockscomb. He usually carried in his hand the sceptre of his office, the bauble, which was a stick ornamented with a fool's head at the end, to which was often attached the inflated bladder for the purpose of belabouring his enemies. Some fools carried a dagger of lath as well or instead. (Douce, *Illustrations of Shakespeare*, ii. 317); 2. 7. 13, 17, 29, etc.

NAMES. The general sense is clear (v. note), though the precise meaning is uncertain. Furness quotes from Cooper's *Thesaurus*, 1573, the best-known dictionary of the day, 'nomina, the names of debtes owen'; 2. 5. 20

NATURAL, idiot; 1. 2. 50

NATURAL PHILOSOPHER, (a) scientist, esp. physicist, (b) Touchstone also glances at 'natural' = idiot, whose philosophy would be profound; 3. 2. 30

NAUGHT, (i) worthless, useless; 1. 2. 62; 3. 2. 15; (ii) 'be naught,' i.e. keep quiet, shut up, make yourself scarce; 1. 1. 33

NEW-FANGLED, carried away by novelty, giddy-pated; 4. 1. 147

OBSERVANCE, respectful attention; 3. 2. 232; 5. 2. 92

OCCASION, 'an opportunity of attacking, of fault-finding, of giving or taking offence; a "handle" against a person' (N.E.D. 'occasion' I. 1); 4. 1. 169

ODDS, superiority, advantage (cf. *L.L.L.* 1. 2. 169); 1. 2. 148

PAINTED CLOTH, the commonest and cheapest kind of wall-hanging, generally representing some tale or sentimental theme —'a pretty slight drollery, or the story of the Prodigal, or the German hunting in waterwork' (2 *Hen. IV*, 2. 1. 156–58)— with verses to match; 3. 2. 271

PAIR OF STAIRS, a flight of stairs ('pair' = set); 5. 2. 36

PANCAKE. The word 'pancake' in the 16th and 17th cent. was equivalent to 'fritter' or 'flap-jack'; N.E.D. ('fritter' sb. 1) quotes Taylor the Water-Poet (1634): 'pancake or fritter or flapiacke.' Now meat-fritters might very well be eaten with mustard; 1. 2. 60

PANTALOON, orig. a stock figure of the Italian comic stage, representing Venice, and shown as a lean, foolish and vicious old man, wearing spectacles, hose and slippers (v. N.E.D. 'pantaloon' 1 a); hence 'a dotard, an old fool'; 2. 7. 158

PARCELS (IN), in detail, piece-meal; 3. 5. 124

PART, depart from; 2. 1. 51

PATHETICAL, passion-moving; 4. 1. 187

PLACES, texts, extracts, short passages from books (v. N.E.D. 7 *b*). The word can also mean 'topics or subjects of discourse,' which is the sense generally accepted; but this does not suit so well with 'vents in mangled forms'; 2. 7. 40

POINT-DEVICE, perfectly correct, very precise; 3. 2. 373

POLITIC, cunning, scheming; 5. 4. 44

PRACTICE, plot; 2. 3. 26

PRESENTATION, semblance; 5. 4. 104

PRIME, (*a*) spring-time, (*b*) the choicest quality; 5. 3. 35

PRINT (IN), precisely—with a quibble upon the orig. meaning; 5. 4. 88

PRIZER, prize-fighter; 2. 3. 8

PROFIT, progress in learning (cf. *Temp.* 1. 2. 172 'Have I, thy schoolmaster, made thee more profit'); 1. 1. 6

PROPER, handsome; 1. 2. 112; 3. 5. 51, 115

PUNY, lit. junior, hence 'a puny tilter' = a young or inexperienced tilter; 3. 4. 41

PUKE, vomit; 2. 7. 144

PURCHASE, acquire; 3. 2. 337

PURGATION, (*a*) theol. 'clearing from guilt,' (*b*) medicinal purging; 1. 3. 53; 5. 4. 43

PURLIEU, 'a piece or tract of land on the fringe or border of a forest' (N.E.D.). This is the orig. meaning of the word; 4. 3. 76

PUT ON, pass off (something unwelcome) upon a person, force something upon one; 1. 2. 88

PYTHAGORAS, the Greek philosopher who preached the doctrine of the transmigration of souls; 3. 2. 177

QUAIL, slacken, become feeble (the orig. sense); 2. 2. 20

QUESTION, talk, conversation (a common meaning with Shakespeare; cf. *unquestionable*); 3. 4. 34; 5. 4. 158

QUINTAIN, a wooden figure at which to tilt. 'It was generally made in the likeness of a Turk or Saracen, armed at all points, bearing a shield upon his left arm, and brandishing a club or sabre with his right' (Strutt, *Sports and Pastimes*); 1. 2. 239

QUINTESSENCE, 'the "fifth essence" of ancient and mediaeval philosophy, supposed to be the substance of which the heavenly bodies were composed, and to be actually latent in all things, the extraction of it by distillation or other methods being one of the great objects of alchemy' (N.E.D.); 3 2. 139

QUIP, sharp retort, sarcastic remark; 5. 4. 74, 91

QUOTIDIAN, a continuous fever or ague, as distinguished from the intermittent kinds; 3. 2. 357

RANKNESS, luxuriance of growth; 1. 1. 82

RASCAL, rabble, often used as a collective term for 'the young, lean or inferior deer of a herd, distinguished from the full-grown antlered bucks or stags' (N.E.D.); but Shakespeare appears to have used the term in the unusual sense of 'a deer with a great head and a small body, who would neither fight

nor run' (cf. *Cor.* 1. 1. 163 and
Sh. Eng. ii. 339 *n.*); 3. 3. 54

RECOUNTMENT, relation, recital
(N.E.D. quotes no other instance); 4. 3. 140

RELIGIOUS, i.e. member of a religious order; 3. 2. 339; 5. 4.
157

RELISH, make pleasant to the
palate (e.g. by adding sauce); 3.
2. 232

REMORSE, pity, compassion; 1. 3. 70

ROYNISH, scurvy, base; 2. 2. 8

SAD, serious; 3. 2. 212

SALE-WORK, 'ready-made goods'
(Wright); N.E.D. quotes 1775
Ash, *Saleswork*, work done for
sales, work slightly performed;
3. 5. 43

SCHOOL, university; 1. 1. 5

SCRIP, (a) wallet or satchel, such
as shepherds, beggars and fools
wore, (b) small piece of paper
(perhaps the usual term for
stage-paper; cf. *M.N.D.* 1. 2. 3
'according to the scrip'); 3. 2.
163

SEAL up, make up (one's mind); 4.
3. 58

SEARCH (A WOUND), probe; 2. 4. 43

SEEMING, seemly; 5. 4. 68

SEIZE, take possession of according
to legal procedure; 3. 1. 10

SENTENTIOUS, full of pithy sayings;
5. 4. 62

SEQUESTERED, excommunicated, cut
off from one's fellows; 2. 1. 33

SHAKE UP, rate soundly, abuse
violently ('very common in the
16–17th cent.' N.E.D.); 1. 1. 26

SIMPLE, ingredient in medicine
(not necessarily a herb, though
by a natural process the word
came to be identified with that
sense); 4. 1. 16

SIR ('Sir Oliver Martext'). This
title was commonly prefixed to
the Christian names of ordinary
priests in medieval times, but
later came to be used in con-
trast to 'Master' and denoted
a priest or minister who had
not graduated at the university
(v. N.E.D. 'sir' 4 and *Sh. Eng.*
i. 59); 3. 3. 40

SLUT, (a) slattern, (b) a loose
woman; 3. 3. 32–5

SMOTHER, the dense smoke produced by a fire without flame;
1. 2. 275

SORT, class, rank; 1. 1. 156

SPLEEN, impulse, waywardness;
4. 1. 207

SQUAND'RING, stray, straggling,
lavishly distributed; 2. 7. 57

STALKING-HORSE, i.e. an old horse
or ox, or a canvas imitation of
the same, behind which the
fowler lurked so as to get close
up to the game (v. *Sh. Eng.* ii.
372 for an excellent illustration
of 'stalking'); 5. 4. 103

STANZO, stanza. The word, a new
importation, seems to have
been regarded as affected by
Shakespeare, who puts it into
the mouth of Holofernes in
L.L.L. (4. 2. 110); 2. 5. 17

STING, sexual appetite; 2. 7. 66

SUN ('to live i'th' sun'). Usually
interpreted 'to live a free open-
air life,' but *Ham.* 1. 2. 67 'I
am too much i'th' sun' suggests
a less obvious meaning. N.E.D.
connects it with the proverbial
phrase 'out of God's blessing
into the warm sun,' which referring originally no doubt to
the passing of a congregation
out of church, came to denote
any change for the worse in

one's condition. The idea of
outlawry, exclusion from society,
would readily attach itself to
the phrase, and would suit both
contexts excellently. We interpret it therefore as 'to live the
life of an outlaw'; 2. 5. 37

SWASHING, swaggering, dashing;
1. 3. 120

SWAY, control (in the astrological
sense); 3. 2. 4

TAKE UP (A QUARREL), make up,
settle; 5. 4. 47, 96

TAX, censure, blame; 2. 7. 71, 86;
3. 2. 344

TAXATION, satire, censure; 1. 2. 79

TEMPER, compound, mix, 'blend
together the ingredients of a
compound' (Wright); 1. 2. 11

TENDER, regard, value; 5. 2. 67

THRASONICAL, boastful, like Thraso
the braggart soldier in Terence's
Eunuchus; 5. 2. 30

TOUCH (i.e. with the pencil or
brush), trait; 3. 2. 152; 5. 4. 27

TOUCHED, tainted; 3. 2. 343

TOY, trifle; 3. 3. 73

TURN, fashion or shape a work of
art, a poem, a tune or a compliment; 2. 5. 3

TURN INTO, bring into; 4. 3. 23

UMBER, a brown earth used as a
pigment; 1. 3. 112

UNBANDED, without a hatband; 3.
2. 370

UNDERHAND, quiet, not obvious,
unobtrusive; 1. 1. 132

UNEXPRESSIVE, not to be expressed;
3. 2. 10

UNQUESTIONABLE, taciturn, averse
to conversation (N.E.D. ex-
plains as 'not submitting to
question, impatient,' but cf.
question and *Ham.* 1. 4. 43
'questionable'); 3. 2. 366

USE, profit, benefit; 2. 1. 12

VENGEANCE, mischief, harm; 4. 3.
48

WARE, (a) aware, (b) cautious; 2.
4. 55, 56

WARP, (a) cause to shrink or cor-
rugate; 2. 7. 187; (b) go astray
from the straight path; 3. 3.
83

WEARING, wearying (cf. *All's Well*,
5. 1. 4); 2. 4. 37

WELL SAID! well done! 2. 6. 14

WORKING, endeavour; 1. 2. 192

WRATH OF LOVE, violent passion,
ecstasy of love; 5. 2. 38

ADDENDA

ALLY, Kinsman; 5. 4. 181

CRY OUT ON, denounce; 2. 7. 70

FANG, grip; 2. 1. 6

FRIEND, relative, ancestor; 1. 3. 62

RENDER, report; 4. 3. 122

SOUTH, S.W. wind; 3. 5. 50

WOMAN OF THE WORLD, married
woman; 5. 3. 4

WORDSWORTH CLASSICS

General Editors: Marcus Clapham and Clive Reynard
Other titles in this series—

Distribution

AUSTRALIA, BRUNEI
& MALAYSIA
Treasure Press
22 Salmon Street
Port Melbourne, Vic 3207
Tel: (03) 646 6716
Fax: (03) 646 6925

DENMARK
BOG-FAN
St. Kongensgade 61A
1264 København K

BOGPA SIKA
Industrivej 1
7120 Vejle Ø

FRANCE
Bookking International
16 Rue Des Grands Augustins
75006 Paris, France

GERMANY, AUSTRIA
& SWITZERLAND
Swan Buch-Marketing GmbH
Goldscheuerstrabe 16
D-7640 Kehl Am Rhein
Germany

GREAT BRITAIN & IRELAND
Wordsworth Editions Ltd
8B East Street, Ware
Herts SG12 9HU

Selecta Books
The Selectabook Distribution Centre
Folly Road, Roundway, Devizes
Wilts SN10 2HR

HOLLAND & BELGIUM
Uitgeverlj En Boekhandel
Van Gennep BV
Spuistraat 283
1012 VR Amsterdam, Holland

ITALY
Magis Books
Piazza Della Vittoria 1/C
42100 Reggio Emilia
Tel: 0522-452303
Fax: 0522-452845

NEW ZEALAND
Whitcoulls Limited
Private Bag 92098
Auckland, New Zealand

NORWAY
Norsk Bokimport AS
Bertrand Narvesensvei 2
Postboks 6219, Etterstad
0602 Oslo, Norway

SINGAPORE
Book Station
18 Leo Drive
Singapore
Tel: 4511998
Fax: 4529188

SOUTH AFRICA
Trade Winds Press (Pty) Ltd
P O Box 20194
Durban North 4016
South Africa

SWEDEN
Akademibokhandelsgruppen
Box 21002
100 31 Stockholm